STORM OF EAGLES

STORM OF EAGLES

THE GREATEST AVIATION PHOTOGRAPHS OF WORLD WAR II

JOHN DIBBS & KENT RAMSEY

WITH TEXT BY
LIEUTENANT COLONEL ROBERT RENNER, USAF

CHARTWELL
BOOKS

© 2017 Osprey Publishing, an imprint of Bloomsbury Publishing Plc

This edition published in 2019 by Chartwell Books,
an imprint of The Quarto Group
142 West 36th Street, 4th Floor
New York, NY 10018 USA
www.QuartoKnows.com

Chartwell Books titles are also available at discount for retail, wholesale, promotional, and bulk purchase. For details, contact the Special Sales Manager by email at specialsales@quarto.com or by mail at: The Quarto Group, Attn: Special Sales Manager, 100 Cummings Center Suite 265D, Beverly, MA 01915, USA.

10 9 8 7 6 5 4 3

ISBN: 978-0-7858-3716-9

Book Concept and Design Concept by John Dibbs of
    the Plane Picture Company www.planepicture.com
Photo Restoration by John Dibbs and Kent Ramsey
Index by Zoe Ross
Typeset in Gill Sans
Originated by PDQ Digital Media Solutions, UK

Printed in China

Acknowledgments

The authors would like to thank the following without whose assistance and support this project would not have been possible: Bill Klaers, Mark Earle, Kurt Peterson, Diane Haagensen, Alessandro Taffetani, Iain Dougall, Colonel Steve Pisanos and Jeff Pisanos.

Special thanks to: Jim Slattery, Michael Slattery and the Slattery Family Foundation for making this book possible. Also Pam Dibbs, Brian Denesen and Allan Burney, whose contributions and assistance have proved invaluable. Sadly Colonel Steve Pisanos, who provided the foreword for this book, did not live to see it in print.

This book features the collections of John Dibbs and Kent Ramsey. Kent Ramsey would also like to thank the staff and personnel at the following institutions for their assistance throughout his many years of research: The National Archives and Records Administration, The National Museum of the United States Air Force, The United States Air Force Academy, The Imperial War Museum, The Royal Air Force Museum and The Halesworth Airfield Museum.

John Dibbs

I would like to dedicate this book to Colonel Clarence "Bud" Anderson whose friendship and support have meant the world to me. I would like to personally thank Pam Dibbs for her dedication to this project.

I also could not have done this book without the support of Luigino Caliaro, Masa Takumi, Shigeru Nohara, Alessandro Metellini, Michel Benichou, Tony Holmes and Phil Jarrett.

A very special thank you to Kirby Milton who has made available his collection of amazing color photography for the production, also a special thanks to Kate Moore at Osprey Publishing for her like-minded passion for the subject and commitment to creating this book.

Kent Ramsey

I would like to dedicate this book to Captain John G. Austin (my uncle) and all of the other brave pilots of World War II who paid the ultimate sacrifice for their countries. It is my express hope that these images will keep their spirits alive for future generations.

Special thanks to Lieutenant Colonel Harry Trimble for igniting my interest in collecting aviation images and to Stan Piet for all of his sage advice on World War II photography.

Lastly, I would like to thank my wife Mimi for all of her patience and to John Dibbs for making this "dream book" a reality.

Robert "Cricket" Renner

Although many people have a misconception of fighter pilots as being arrogant, one thing I have found in common among fighter pilots of all wars and all generations is their humility. Every fighter pilot who fought in World War II says, "I am no hero. I was just doing my job." I would like to thank all those brave men for "just doing their jobs" so we can enjoy the fresh air of freedom today.

I would also like to thank John "Dibbsy" Dibbs for the vision on this project, as well as providing a great name for my new puppy! Most importantly, I want to thank Conny for her patience, encouragement and support.

CONTENTS

FOREWORD

I came to the United States because I wanted to become an aviator. While growing up in Greece, that is all I wanted to be. When my home country was overrun by Hitler's Nazi army, I was determined to carry on the fight as an aviator against the Germans. With the few dollars I was making from "bussing" tables in Plainfield, New Jersey, I learned to fly, using what money was left to take classes in English. These were desperate times and my compulsion to act was overwhelming.

With my pilot's license in my pocket, I volunteered to fight with the British Royal Air Force, as America had yet to enter the war. Following the Japanese attack on Pearl Harbor, American forces were deployed to the European Theater and the conflict became global. As the Americans developed their fledgling Air Force in England, I was transferred to the USAAF, where, flying Spitfires, Thunderbolts and Mustangs, I bore witness to some of the most amazing sights and sounds that anyone could have experienced.

The Second World War was the largest and most expensive conflict in history, in terms of human life and matériel. Battles on land, sea and air took place across the expanse of the globe, and affected everyone on the entire planet. The air campaign was notable because it was the first time air power was exercised both tactically and strategically in warfare, some battles being settled by aircraft alone for the first time in history. The scale reached during the conflict of 1939–45 is still almost unimaginable.

It has often been said that war is both the worst and best of times for those involved. War, without a doubt, changes the lives of those involved forever, and the consequences of such an event far outlive those who fought, survived or died in the name of their country. The scars and effects of war are permanent.

One of my most memorable moments was when I lost the engine in my P-51. After receiving flak damage over Le Havre, I decided to head south and bail out over the countryside. I had reached 3,000ft in altitude and estimated that I was some 20–25km or more south of Le Havre. I trimmed the Mustang to fly hands-off and, surprisingly, it did very well. I then released the safety harness, got rid of my helmet and gloves, and opened the canopy using the emergency handle. However, as I struggled to stand up, attempting to step out on the wing, I felt something holding me back. I looked down and saw that the dinghy cord, which was attached to my Mae West, was probably jammed somewhere behind the pilot's seat.

Sitting back in the cockpit, I tried, again, to free the trapped cord by pulling it as hard as I could, but the metal plug at the end of the cord, wherever it was jammed behind the seat, would not give. I began to sweat with fear from the entanglement I had found myself in, being in an aircraft with a dead engine, about to crash in enemy territory. My instinct was telling me not to give up, as I tried pulling the cord once more. I moved it to the left and right. I twisted it and played with the cord by juggling it from one side to the other and, suddenly, the unexpected happened. "A miracle," I thought. The jammed plug at the end of the cord was free! I stepped out on the wing while holding onto the canopy rail, and was just about ready to let go and slide down the wing to freedom, when I looked around and realized that I was now too close to the ground to bail out.

Suddenly, fright and tremor confronted me when I saw that the dead-engined Mustang was gliding down, straight towards the roof of a barn adjacent to the only farmhouse in the area. As the aircraft got closer to the ground, I reached inside the cockpit and pulled the stick back gently with my right hand, causing the Mustang to climb up a bit, barely clearing the barn. This action, of course, killed some of the Mustang's gliding speed as the aircraft headed for the crash.

Many thoughts flashed through my mind at that moment, as I prayed to the Almighty for mercy. I held tightly, using all my strength, to the left longeron near the cockpit – while on my knees – when the right wing tip scraped the ground and the Mustang skidded on its belly along the soft farmland. I was thrown forward and to the left, barely missing the stopped propeller. I never saw the ground racing to meet me as I tumbled in the air with my eyes closed. Although this was only the beginning of the adventure, it was typical of the extraordinary nature of lives entangled in the Second World War.

With the passing of over 70 years since the battles that shaped our present world, and with tensions flaring in the same regions that saw the Second World War take hold, the lessons of what I and my generation experienced seem more poignant than ever.

This is why I recommend this compelling book, *Storm of Eagles*, to those interested in aviation, history and human experience. The beautifully restored photos of the Second World War air campaign are so sharp and vivid that they allow those who were not there to gain a sense of what it was like. The book also supports the National Museum of World War II Aviation in Colorado Springs, Colorado.

John Dibbs and Kent Ramsey have spent almost the same length of time collecting and restoring these images as the war itself lasted. It creates a fitting and lasting legacy to my fellow pilots, as well as the maintainers and engineers who gave their all during this exceptional period of history. Civilization depended on us.

The drama, the flying, the camaraderie and the global nature of the conflict are presented in a way that brings those incredible days back to life. Through this book my yesterday becomes today again.

Colonel Steve N. Pisanos, USAF (Ret)
Ten-victory ace RAF "Eagle" Squadron and USAAF pilot

INTRODUCTION

Storm of Eagles, so named because nearly all the World War II air forces used an eagle in their crests, was born from a comment by a former USAAF fighter ace, Harrison "Bud" Tordoff. It was the day he was reunited with "his" P-51D, one that he flew in combat from England during the war. He had been invited to visit a former training airfield, but didn't know that his fully restored aircraft was concealed in a revetment. When he finally came face-to-face with his actual P-51D named "Upupa Epops," the moment of recognition was something to behold. "Bud" was visibly stunned and moved. There it was, resplendent in the morning light, packed parachute on the tailplane, canopy open, ready to go. Such was its authenticity, that the airliner contrails above could easily have been streaming from B-17s. We left him with his thoughts. Eventually I asked him how he felt. He quipped: "You can't imagine… the last time I saw that airplane it was in black and white."

In that moment the concept for this book was conceived. Why should we have to "imagine?" It dawned on me that scratchy, fuzzy old photographs in books only distance us from the subject, when they intend to do the opposite. I wanted to create a book that was a window through time, no scratches, dust or blur. The men and aircraft of World War II in the crystal clear here and now. But where to start…

Back in the 1930s, Germany's Third Reich recognized that "a photograph is worth a thousand words" and used the power of mass media to feed the National Socialist doctrine to a nation. Initially through mass rallies and radio broadcast, then through books, film and print, lavishly illustrated with dramatic and powerful imagery. Thus, when the German "Blitzkrieg" of Europe began in 1939, war correspondents and photographers were sent into battle alongside the troops. Photography was used as a tool of propaganda, a way to bolster morale, educate, or sometimes mislead, the folks "back home" as to how well the war effort was going. The camera became a weapon and saw action on all fronts during this cataclysmic time. A huge archive of imagery was thus amassed.

War drives huge technological development and this was also true for camera and film. This is clearly evident throughout the chapters in this book. Nearly all the early war images were black and white, and needed basic retouching even back then to reproduce well. Many still carry the subtle paintbrush marks where edges were "sharpened". By the end of the war, Kodak was producing the revolutionary Kodachrome film, and an original 5in x 4in Kodak transparency from 1944, well exposed and archived correctly, produces breathtaking results, as if they were taken yesterday. Thus, the challenge was to find and restore previously unseen aviation images from the conflict.

I have been fortunate enough to have two willing partners in this venture. Kent Ramsey and Robert "Cricket" Renner. Kent and I have spent years hunting down and restoring imagery from the period. Scanning from first-generation copies is a revelation. Some images you may have seen before, but never in this level of detail. Scanned to the highest resolution with every scratch, dust spot and paper wrinkle removed. History becomes reality. You can see the razor bump of the young Fred Christensen, who probably shaved too keenly as he was being photographed by the legendary Ardean Miller III in glorious full color. You can also feel the chill as shipmates stand in the shadow of an aircraft carrier's superstructure, solemnly laying a fallen comrade to rest in a sea burial during the Pacific campaign. Adding insight to the photographs, former USAF fighter pilot "Cricket" Renner researched the images to give substance and depth via his wonderful writing.

Authenticity was our keyword. We wanted the book to look, feel and become "real" to the reader. This book is not intended to be an encyclopedia or history on World War II aviation, but rather a "time-machine." Within these pages we visit a world completely at war, a war in which air power became the decisive tactical and strategic factor in helping win the conflict, where people like "Bud" Tordoff lived life in color. Their bravery, their fear, their joy, and their loss. How they lived and in many cases died. All this before many had seen their twenty-second birthday.

Time passes, but it needn't be history. The more we understand the events of yesteryear, the better we may be equipped to avoid the errors of that time. The best tribute we can pay the "Greatest Generation" is to recognize their vast personal cost, and vow to value our freedom going forward.

John Dibbs

John Dibbs, 2017

PREFACE

The Second World War changed the world forever. The incredible shift in aviation technology during the six years of the conflict still affect our every day. The design, technology and manufacturing of wartime aircraft ultimately created an industry that would shrink the planet, boosting human connections and creating global economies.

It is ironic that machines built to destroy could create so much. Naturally, they could only have this effect if victory was achieved, and it is both these things we commemorate and celebrate at the National Museum of World War II Aviation, based in Colorado Springs.

Our museum is a unique project with education at its heart. This phenomenal period of human history is told through our detailed exhibits and interactive displays along with genuine World War II flying aircraft. The experience of seeing a legendary military aircraft fire up and take to the skies creates an emotional response that is truly inspiring, so therefore keeping these aircraft flying is an integral part of our mission.

The approach of restoring the aircraft of the period is now almost in direct contrast to the wartime "Arsenal of Democracy" of the United States, when huge facilities fed the Allied aviation war machine, producing 300,000 aircraft in 1945 alone. Rebuilding the flyers within our collection is a labor of love now, each hand-crafted, and funded by like-minded individuals who want to share the experience with the greater public as a tribute to the fallen. We aim to educate people on the history of them but back it up with the opportunity to see aircraft being rebuilt, propellers overhauled and powerplants run up today. Our aim is to inspire new generations to be involved with this. We want to illustrate that exceptional can be the norm, and thus commemorate the people that served in the name of liberty, whether that was designing, building or fighting in the incredible aircraft of the era.

The Second World War was a period of human history that is abundant with lessons to learn on many levels, and it is through *Storm of Eagles* that we hope to reach out to a global audience, and bring into sharp focus the time that changed the world for good.

Bill Klaers
President and CEO, National Museum of World War II Aviation

CHAPTER ONE

THE THIRD REICH MOVES ON EUROPE

Our sadly diminished squadron flew to defend one of the [Army] hospitals. Six of us on this occasion found ourselves in a scrap with 40 Junkers 87 Stukas. We shot down 14, and turned the raid away. I brought down a Ju 87 and damaged another. Whilst following him I saw a bigger target, a Dornier 17; after a close encounter, this aircraft caught fire and crashed. Initially I had felt rather satisfied that we had achieved a small but worthwhile victory, but soon after I turned for home I saw a fresh wave of 150 enemy bombers starting out on another raid, and my frustration at our lack of numbers to combat them was intense.

Group Captain Dennis David, RAF, describing his May 11, 1940 fight over France

On the third day of the campaign, May 12, 1940, I managed to score my first kill. During a patrol flight that afternoon I shot down my third opponent out of a formation of five Hurricanes. An excellent weapon and luck had been on my side. To be successful the best fighter pilot needs both.

Generalleutnant Adolf Galland, Luftwaffe, 104-kill ace

World War II – the deadliest and most widespread war in human history – resulted in an estimated 60 million deaths. This "total war" involved the vast majority of the world's nations, with their entire economies, industrial and scientific capabilities supporting the war effort. It also erased the historical distinction between civilian and military resources and targets. The world's air forces began the conflict with propeller-driven aircraft and a misguided belief in the superiority of the bomber, and ended with jet fighters, ballistic missiles and the atomic bomb.

Although generally recognized to have started with Nazi Germany's invasion of Poland, World War II really had its genesis in the end of the Great War in 1918. After four years of bloody trench warfare, including the first wide-scale military use of the airplane, World War I ended with the Treaty of Versailles. It punished Germany particularly harshly, putting on it significant territorial and financial losses. One of the restrictions prohibited Germany from having an air force. The financial reparations helped create a nationalistic sentiment that led to the rise of Adolf Hitler and his Nationalist Socialist German Workers' Party, known as the Nazi Party.

In addition, during the inter-war years, many military strategists looked to airpower as a way to prevent a repeat of the mass casualties of World War I. Several countries refined their airpower doctrine in conflicts shortly before World War II. Italy, under the Fascist leader Mussolini, invaded Ethiopia in 1935. During the Spanish Civil War from 1936–39, Hitler and Mussolini supported General Francisco Franco and his Nationalist rebels, while the USSR supported the Spanish Republic. Both sides used this as a testing ground for their weapons and tactics. Meanwhile, in the Far East, the Sino-Japanese conflict had descended into a full-blown war in 1937 that was to significantly influence events to come.

In March 1938, Germany annexed Austria, and later the Sudetenland (in Czechoslovakia), with little response from other European powers. A year later, Hitler invaded the remainder of Czechoslovakia. Britain and France guaranteed their support for an independent Poland, and later extended that pledge to Romania and Greece. Hitler, however, was working on a secret non-aggression treaty with the Soviet Union, giving each country "spheres of influence" over Eastern Europe. It assured Hitler that he would not face a two-front war.

On September 1, 1939, Hitler attacked Poland and two days later France and the United Kingdom declared war on Germany. Poland was quickly overwhelmed by a new type of warfare the Germans called "blitzkrieg" (lightning war), using air power in support of rapid armored advances. On September 27, Warsaw surrendered, with the final pockets of resistance capitulating on October 6. After Hitler's public peace overture to Britain and France on that same day, British Prime Minister Neville Chamberlain rejected it by stating: "Past experience has shown that no reliance can be placed upon the promises of the present German Government." In response, Hitler ordered an immediate invasion of France, but poor weather and changes to the operational plans forced postponement until the spring of 1940. This led to the winter of 1939–40 being known as the "Phoney War," when there were few land battles and only sporadic fighting between the opposing air forces and navies.

April 1940 saw the German invasion of Denmark and Norway – the former surrendering within a few hours and the latter within two months. On May 10, 1940, Germany launched an all-out offensive against France, as well as the neutral countries of Belgium, the Netherlands and Luxembourg. The very same day, Winston Churchill took over as British Prime Minister. A large segment of the Royal Air Force (RAF) deployed to France as part of the British Expeditionary Force, to help the French defend their country and try to prevent Hitler conquering Western Europe.

In the few fierce weeks of May, British, French and German fighters and bombers tangled in the skies over Europe. The Allies, however, could not stem the tide of the German Wehrmacht and Luftwaffe, and by early June, the Allied armies were defeated, captured, or being evacuated at Dunkirk. Paris fell on June 14, and on June 22, the French signed an armistice. Now, Germany and Italy controlled the European continent. Only Britain remained standing against them.

 Luftwaffe Messerschmitt Bf 109B, Germany, 1938. Introduced into service in 1937, the Messerschmitt Bf 109 first saw combat in the Spanish Civil War. It was the main Luftwaffe fighter at the beginning of World War II and remained a competitive fighter until the end of the conflict. Flown by most of Germany's top aces, almost 34,000 examples were built, making it the most produced fighter in history.

 Luftwaffe Heinkel He 111H-6, Germany, 1938. First flown in 1935 and produced until September 1944, the He 111 was the most numerous Luftwaffe bomber at the start of World War II. With their unique "greenhouse" nose, He 111s served as medium bombers until 1943 when they were relegated to a transport role.

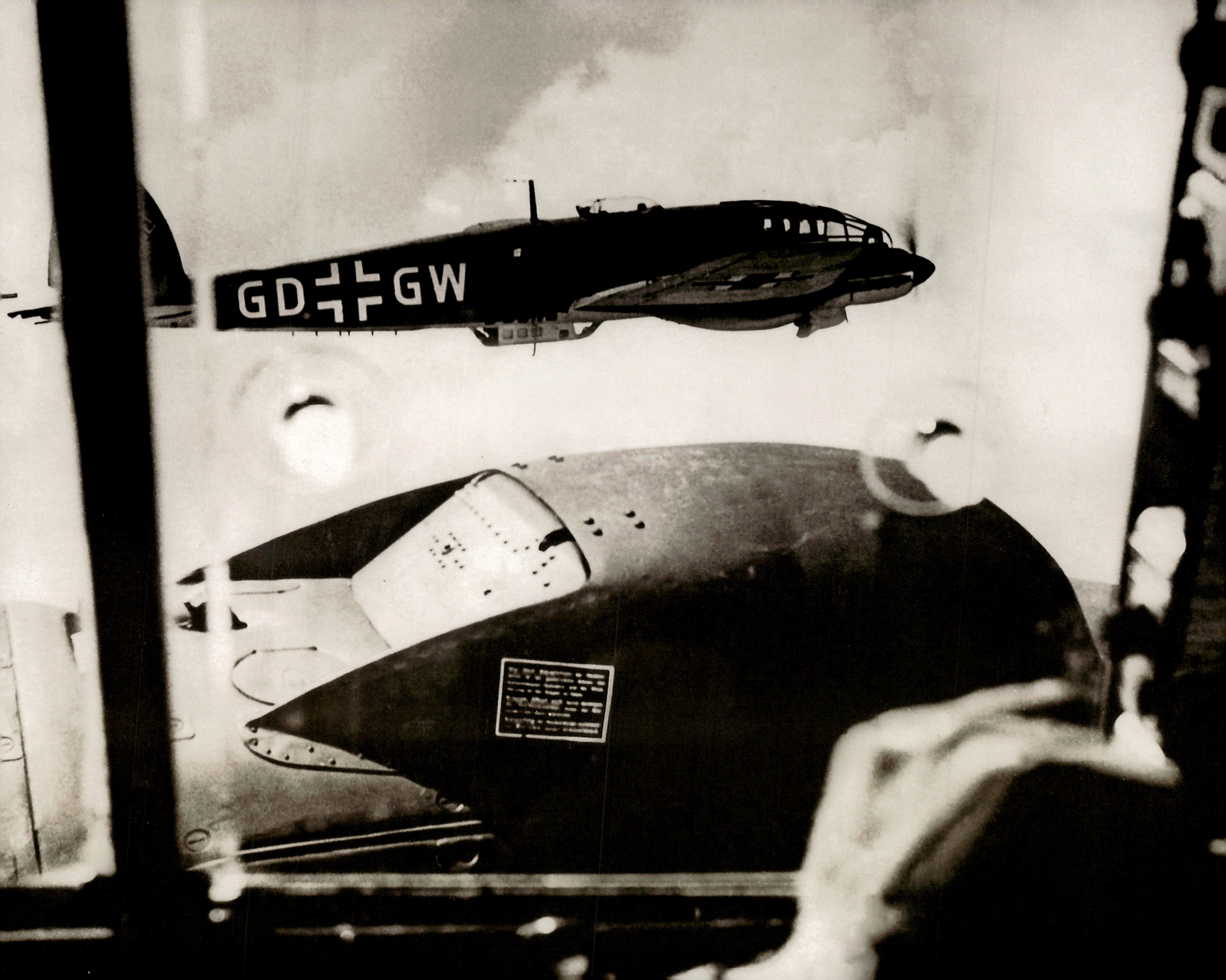
GD GW

 **Luftwaffe Junkers Ju 87, Germany, 1939.** First used during the Spanish Civil War by the Luftwaffe's Condor Legion, the Ju 87 Stuka (from *Sturzkampfflugzeug*, meaning dive bomber), became the propaganda symbol of the German Blitzkrieg. Used to great effect during the invasion of Poland in September 1939, they would play a key role in the rapid conquest of Western Europe during 1940.

Luftwaffe Messerschmitt Bf 109E, Germany, 1939. The Bf 109E was a much-improved version of the nimble fighter, with a 20mm cannon firing through the propeller spinner, as well as a 20mm cannon in each wing.

Polish AF PZL P.11a, Poland, 1939. Designed in the early 1930s, the P.11 was the primary Polish fighter at the outbreak of the war. Greatly outclassed by the Luftwaffe's more advanced aircraft, the Polish fighter pilots fought valiantly – claiming 110 victories for the loss of 100 P.11s. A P.11c was the first aircraft shot down in World War II (by a Stuka), and 20 minutes later, 2nd Lt Wladyslaw Gnys in a P.11c achieved the first Allied air victory when he shot down two Dornier Do 17 bombers. This P.11a belongs to the 113th Fighter Escadrille based at Okecie, Warsaw.

 Luftwaffe Dornier Do 17, Western Front, winter 1939. Nicknamed the "Flying Pencil" for its long, narrow fuselage, the Dornier Do 17 was a medium bomber designed in the early 1930s. As one of two main Luftwaffe bombers at the start of the war, it saw extensive service in every major campaign until late 1941. Production of the Do 17 ended in mid-1940 after 2,139 had been built.

 RAF Fairey Battle, England, early 1939. Caught in the transition from the biplane, the RAF Fairey Battle light bomber was advanced when designed in 1934 but obsolete by the time of its first flight in 1936. Ironically, on September 20, 1939, a Battle shot down a German Bf 109, achieving the first RAF air-to-air kill of the war. However, when the German assault on France began on May 10, 1940, 60 out of 108 Battles sent on missions were shot down over a period of five days.

 RAF Bristol Blenheim Mk IF, England, 1939. Designed in the mid 1930s as a light bomber, the
Bristol Blenheim also served in the RAF as a night fighter. However, by the time World War II
began, it was mostly obsolete, with Blenheim units suffering heavy casualties.

 Luftwaffe Heinkel He 111, Germany, 1940.
Heinkel He 111 bomber crews about to
board their aircraft.

 Luftwaffe Messerschmitt Bf 109E, Germany, 1939. A Bf 109E-1
of the Luftwaffe's IV./JG 51. This *Jagdgeschwader* (fighter wing) was
in combat for the entire duration of the war. Its pilots won more
awards than any other *Jagdgeschwader*.

Hptm Wilhelm Balthasar

21

 French AF Morane-Saulnier MS.406C-1, France, 1940. The MS.406 was France's most numerous fighter at the start of World War II. Outclassed by the Luftwaffe's Bf 109E, the *Armée de l'Air*'s MS.406 was maneuverable but slow and had insufficient armament as well as an antiquated gunsight (the long tube protruding from the windscreen). Approximately 400 MS.406s were lost between May 10 and June 25, 1940. After the fall of France, the MS.406 continued to serve the Vichy French in Syria, as well as the German, Croatian and Finnish Air Forces.

 Luftwaffe Heinkel He 111, Western Front, 1940. The burnt-out remains of a German He 111 medium bomber that went down on March 12, 1940 in "No Man's Land" during the "Phoney War."

CHAPTER TWO

BATTLE FOR BRITAIN

My first sortie against England will remain in my memory forever… north of Dover we spotted three Spitfires below, with more machines coming out of the fog. We attacked these three first and I put one of them on fire. Meanwhile, however, I found myself among eight or ten Englishmen who seemed angry at me… [My] radiator and fuel tank were hit and I had no choice but to run in a dive for the Channel at 700km/h. The whole gang followed me like a waterfall.

Oberst Werner Mölders, Luftwaffe, 115-kill ace

We were not without fear. The fellow who wasn't didn't live long. And taking a Spitfire into the sky in September of 1940 often corresponded to entering a dark room with a madman waving a knife behind your back. We couldn't see behind us and the Hun was everywhere, ready to spit his guns. Yet fear and intense physical danger and the discomfort of battle were more than compensated by the very positive feelings nearly all of us had of satisfaction at being the only human beings who were able to stand between Hitler and world freedom.

Group Captain A. G. "Sailor" Malan, RAF, 27-kill ace

During the Battle of France, RAF Air Chief Marshal Hugh Dowding sent a letter to his superiors on May 16, 1940, stating: "I believe that… if the Home Defence Force is drained away in desperate attempts to remedy the situation in France, defeat in France will involve the final, complete and irremediable defeat of this country."

Realizing the grim situation on the continent, the RAF began preparing for the next fight against the Germans, a fight for Britain's very existence.

On June 18, 1940 in the House of Commons, British Prime Minister Winston Churchill's words rang through the halls: "…the Battle of France is over. The Battle of Britain is about to begin. Upon this battle depends the survival of Christian civilization, upon it depends our own British life… Let us therefore brace ourselves to our duties, and so bear ourselves that, if the British Empire and its Commonwealth last for a thousand years, men will still say, 'This was their finest hour'."

The Battle of Britain, from July 10 to October 31, 1940, was the first major campaign fought entirely by air forces. In general terms, the battle can be broken down into five phases: Nuisance raids by the Luftwaffe (June 26–July 16); attacks on British channel shipping (July 17–August 12); main assault on RAF airfields (August 13–September 6); day and night bombing of London (September 7–October 2); large scale night bombing of British cities (October 3–31).

Although outnumbered approximately four to one in both aircraft and pilots, the RAF had radar – a technological advantage that gave them early warning of the Luftwaffe attacks. In addition, they had the psychological advantage of defending their homeland.

Learning from their experiences in the Spanish Civil War, Poland, and France, the Luftwaffe fighter pilots flew in a loose "finger four" formation so that all four pilots could freely search the skies for enemy aircraft and protect each other's tails. However, the Bf 109 escort fighters were limited on fuel, giving them a short time over Britain to protect their bombers from the RAF. Fighter Command, on the other hand, emphasized rigid by-the-book attacks with outdated "Vic" close formations of three aircraft. To intercept the incoming German aircraft, these young RAF fighter pilots (average age of 20) scrambled in their Hurricanes and Spitfires, often up to six times per day.

The RAF's No 11 Group was responsible for the defense of the southeast of England and bore the brunt of the German attacks. Air Vice-Marshal Keith Park launched squadrons one at a time, subjecting the bombers to continual attacks. Arguing for a different tactic, No 12 Group's Air Vice Marshal Trafford Leigh-Mallory, along with legless ace Squadron Leader Douglas Bader, proposed the "Big Wing," in which at least three squadrons would form up to attack the enemy en masse. The debate over which tactic was more effective continues to this day.

On September 15, 1940 (now celebrated as Battle of Britain Day), two massive waves of German bombers were repulsed by the RAF. Sixty German aircraft were shot down, while the RAF lost 26 aircraft. Two days later, Hitler indefinitely postponed his plans to invade Britain.

Of the 2,936 RAF aircrew from 15 nations, 544 lost their lives in the battle and a further 814 died before the end of the war. The Germans suffered 2,585 aircrew killed or missing, with another 925 captured.

The exploits of the RAF's fighter pilots in 1940 were forever immortalized by Churchill's famous speech: "The gratitude of every home in our Empire, and indeed throughout the world except in the abodes of the guilty, goes out to the British airmen, who, undaunted by odds, unwearied in their constant challenge and mortal danger, are turning the tide of world war by their prowess and by their devotion. Never in the field of human conflict was so much owed by so many to so few."

Although the Battle of Britain was over by the end of October, the battle for Britain raged for many more months as Luftwaffe bombers engaged in the Blitz. Until the arrival of the American Air Forces in late 1942, the only Allied offensive against the German armed forces and industry in Western Europe was flown by the RAF pilots of Bomber Command in obsolete bombers on night raids and the daytime Fighter Command sweeps into France.

 Luftwaffe Heinkel He 111H, Scotland, 1939. Shot down by Flying Officer Archie McKellar of No 602 (City of Glasgow) Squadron on October 28, this bomber from Kampfgeschwader 26 was the first German aircraft to crash-land on British soil in World War II. Two of its crew (pilot Kurt Lehmkuhl and navigator Rolf Niehoff) were wounded and captured, but radio operator Bruno Reimann and flight engineer Gottlieb Kowalke were both killed. McKellar would go on to score 21 victories, but was killed in a dogfight with a Bf 109 on November 1, 1940.

 RAF Supermarine Spitfire Mk I, Scotland, 1940. Squadron Leader Andrew D. Farquhar led No 602 (City of Glasgow) Squadron into their first air battle on October 16, 1939. Four months later he shared in shooting down a Heinkel He 111 and then attempted to land next to it to prevent the crew setting fire to their aircraft. Upon landing on soft ground, however, the Spitfire flipped onto its back and Farquhar had to be pulled out by the German bomber crew!

 Luftwaffe Heinkel He 111H, Humbie, Scotland, 1939. Squadron Leader Farquhar examines the bomber brought down by Flg Off Archie McKellar of his squadron.

 RAF Supermarine Spitfire Mk Ia, RAF Duxford, 1939. No 19 Squadron was the first RAF unit to receive the Spitfire in August 1938. These early versions of the British air superiority fighter had a wooden two-blade propeller and several of them still had the flat canopy. At the beginning of the Battle of Britain on July 10, 1940, the RAF had 19 squadrons of Spitfires in addition to its 32 squadrons of Hurricanes.

 RAF Hawker Hurricane Mk I, RAF Tangmere, July 1940. Photographer Charles E. Brown captured the hectic moments between sorties for the pilots and ground crews of No 601 (County of London) Squadron, as their aircraft are refueled and rearmed. Squadron Leader Max Aitken (on the far left) scored 16 aerial victories while flying Hurricanes during the Battle of Britain and Blenheim IF and Beaufighter night fighters later in the war.

 Luftwaffe Junkers Ju 88, France, 1940. Luftwaffe air and ground crew of a Ju 88 *Kampfgeschwader* (bomber wing) commemorate their 2,000th mission in France during the Battle of Britain. Note the map of England on the left post and the map of France on the right.

 RAF Handley Page Hampden, England, September 1941. Three RAF Hampden medium bombers of No 44 Squadron caught over England by the RAF's official photographer, Flying Officer Bertrand Daventry. Almost half of all Hampdens built were lost on operations. The closest aircraft was lost on a raid to Bremen, Germany, on October 21, 1942, killing all four crew, while the middle bomber was shot down over Hamburg, Germany, on July 26, 1942, with the loss of three of its crew. RAF Bomber Command retired the type from service in late 1942.

Oblt Johannes Steinhoff

 Luftwaffe Messerschmitt Bf 109E, France, 1940. "Yellow 10" of Jagdgeschwader 2 having crash landed after engine failure. It has already been salvaged for parts, as both its cannon from the wings and above the engine have been removed.

 RAF Supermarine Spitfire Mk I, Gravesend, England, September 10, 1940. Squadron Leader Rupert "Lucky" Leigh, No 66 Squadron commander from April to October 1940, climbs into his Spitfire. Leigh was credited with one He 111 destroyed and two shared. American Pilot Officer Hugh Reilley was shot down in this aircraft on October 17, 1940, by Luftwaffe ace Werner Mölders.

 Luftwaffe Heinkel He 111, France, 1940. A Luftwaffe bomber taxis out for another sortie against England.

 Luftwaffe Messerschmitt Bf 110C, France, May 1940. A twin-engine heavy fighter, the Bf 110 saw success in the early campaigns of World War II, but its poor maneuverability resulted in devastating losses against RAF fighters in the summer of 1940.

 Luftwaffe Junkers Ju 88, Germany, 1940. Originally developed in 1936 the Ju 88 proved to be an extremely versatile bomber for the Luftwaffe. Over 15,000 were produced.

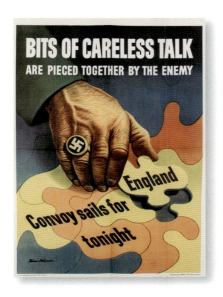

RAF Short Sunderland Mk IIIa, Lough Erne, Northern Ireland, date unknown. The Sunderland long-range patrol bomber was crucial in countering the German U-boats in the Battle of the Atlantic. Nicknamed the "Flying Porcupine" by the Germans owing to its defensive firepower, the Sunderland and its crew of up to 11 could fly 14-hour patrols to drop bombs and depth charges on enemy submarines.

Luftwaffe Heinkel He 111, London, September 7, 1940. Frustrated with the inability to win air superiority over Britain, and to seek revenge for increased British bombing of German cities, Hitler directed the Luftwaffe to change from attacking RAF airfields and aircraft factories to bombing British cities. Flying over the East End of London, this German bomber is about to drop its deadly cargo on the first day of the Blitz.

Danger UXB, London, 1941. The Blitz brought a new term to the British — UXB, for Unexploded Bomb. UXBs from World War II are still routinely found in Britain.

 London, September 1940. The Luftwaffe transitioned from bombing RAF airfields and radar stations to the Blitz (the bombing of London and other British cities) with the raid of September 7, 1940. London was bombed for 57 consecutive days in September and October 1940, and fire consumed huge portions of the city. Many residents sought shelter during the air raids in the Underground stations.

 France, 1940. In time-honored fashion, two Luftwaffe aces talk tactics with their hands. On the left is Major Werner Mölders, the first pilot in history to shoot down 100 aircraft. He died on November 22, 1941 when the He 111 he was a passenger in crashed. Major Adolf Galland, on the right, scored 104 victories in World War II and survived the conflict.

 Messerschmitt Bf 109E-3, Caffers Airfield (Calais) France, August 1940. One of the color photographs taken by JG 26's Hauptmann Rolf Schödter of Leutnant Walter Blume's Bf 109E in the first two weeks of August 1940. The four victory bars on the rudder date this picture between Blume's fourth kill on July 25 and his fifth kill on August 15. He would score again on August 16, but then was shot down by Hurricanes of No 32 Squadron on August 18 and crash landed near Canterbury. Seriously wounded, he was repatriated in 1943 and remarkably returned to combat in 1944, scoring a further eight aerial victories.

 RAF Westland Whirlwind, England, 1942. With the punch of four 20mm cannon in the nose, a bubble canopy for good all-around visibility, and superb maneuverability, the RAF had high hopes for the Whirlwind. However, its limited range and teething problems with its engines resulted in the Whirlwind only serving with two squadrons before it was replaced in November 1943 by the Hawker Typhoon.

 RAF Supermarine Spitfire Mk I, RAF Manston, England, February 6, 1941. Although the Battle of Britian "officially" ended on October 31, 1940, the fighting continued over the Western Front as RAF fighters began taking the war to the Luftwaffe. Here, No 92 (East India) Squadron celebrates the unit's 130th confirmed victory. Of the 10 pilots in the picture, eight survived the war and several became aces. In the center are famous fighter leaders Brian Kingcome (stone-faced) and Johnny Kent, a Canadian (holding the sign). Pilot Officer Roy Mottram (third from left) was shot down and killed on August 31, 1941 while escorting Blenheim bombers on a mission to France. Pilot Officer John Lund (far right) and his two wingmen were shot down by Fw 190s on October 2, 1941 over the English Channel.

 Luftwaffe Junkers Ju 87 Stuka, England, February 20, 1941. RAF fighter pilots of No 92 Squadron examine a Ju 87 Stuka that they have just shot down. Flying Officer Cecil Saunders (far left) and Pilot Officer Ronnie Fokes (far right) were credited with the kill. Both were aces, Saunders surviving the war, but Fokes was killed on June 12, 1944 while bailing out of a Typhoon over France.

 RAF Supermarine Spitfire ASR II,
Warmwell, England, April 1943. Converted
from a Spitfire Mk IIa to an Air Sea Rescue
(ASR) II, this No 276 Squadron aircraft
carried a liferaft, flares and smoke bombs.

 RAF Bristol Beaufighter, southwest
England, 1941. A twin-engined derivative
of the Beaufort bomber, the Beaufighter (or
"Beau" to its crews) served as a night fighter,
ground attack, and maritime strike aircraft.

 RAF Hawker Hurricane, Kirton-in-Lindsey, England, March 17,
1941. Formed on September 19, 1940, No 71 "Eagle" Squadron
was the first of three RAF "Eagle" units to be manned by
American pilots. Friends from California before the war, Andy
Mamedoff (fifth from left, with moustache) and Eugene "Red"
Tobin (sixth from left), were two of the 11 Americans who flew
for RAF Fighter Command in the Battle of Britain. Tragically
neither survived the war. On September 7, 1941, Tobin was shot
down by a Bf 109 of JG 26 over France. Mamedoff died in a
Hurricane crash in bad weather on October 8, 1941.

"CAN ONE THINK, WHILE
FLOWERS BLOOM,
AND FIELDS ARE RICH WITH CORN,
THAT AUGHT SHALL SPOIL
THE LAND WE LOVE---
THE LAND WHERE WE WERE BORN?

RAF Westland Lysander, England, 1942.
Originally designed as an army co-operation aircraft and light bomber, the Westland Lysander suffered devastating losses in the Battle of France – 118 out of the 175 deployed were lost in May–June 1940. In August 1941, however, a new squadron was formed utilizing the Lysander's excellent short-field capabilities to fly clandestine missions to mainland Europe to make contact with the French Resistance.

RAF Douglas A-20 Boston, British factory, September 5, 1942. Female British factory workers join their colleagues to repair an RAF Boston medium bomber.

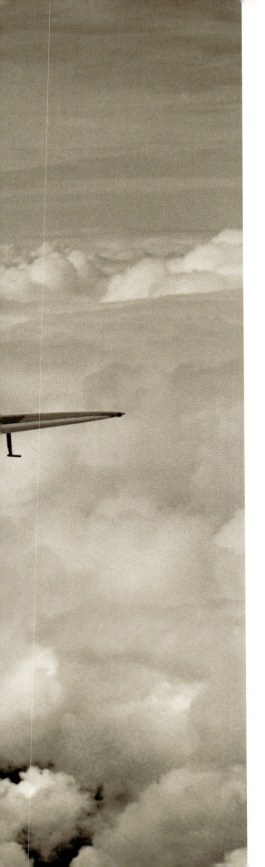

 RAF Supermarine Spitfire Mk IX, RAF Biggin Hill, England, January 3, 1943. Group Captain Adolph "Sailor" Malan (right), station commander, talks to Flight Sergeant Vincent Bunting. Malan led No 74 Squadron during the Battle of Britain and was one of the RAF's most highly decorated fighter pilots with 27 kills. Bunting, a Jamaican, flew Spitfires and Mustangs for the RAF and shot down a Focke-Wulf Fw 190 over Germany on March 27, 1945.

 RAF Supermarine Spitfire Mk Vb, England, 1942. Delivered to No 243 (F) Squadron on June 27, 1942, this Spitfire flew with the unit in England until October 1942. It was eventually transferred to 808 NAS of the Fleet Air Arm. Sub Lieutenant Hugh A. Cogill flew it on June 6, 1944 over the Normandy invasion beaches, but was shot down by an enemy aircraft. Although the 20-year-old tried to bail out, he was killed when the aircraft hit the sea.

CHAPTER THREE

THE BEAR IN THE EAST

After August 1943, the supremacy in the air finally went over to the Soviet pilots and, by the end of the war, we were locking horns with hastily trained youths more and more often. The one-time conceit of invincibility claimed by Göring's aces had gone up in smoke.

Major Ivan Kozhedub, top Soviet ace with 62 victories

Often there were ten of us against 300 Russians. Those are long odds. A mid-air collision was almost as likely as being shot down, too. We had to plan our attacks against these hordes with great care or we never would have survived.

Major Erich Hartmann, top Luftwaffe ace with 352 victories

As part of the Soviet non-aggression pact with Germany, Finland came under the Soviet sphere of influence. However, in 1939, the Soviet Union sought to push its border with Finland on the Karelian Isthmus westward in an attempt to buttress the security of Leningrad from potential German attack. When the Finnish rejected these demands, the Soviets invaded on November 30, 1939 in the start of the Winter War. Despite an overwhelming Soviet superiority in tanks and aircraft, the tenacious Finns held out until signing a peace treaty in March 1940. In a curious political twist, Finland became an ally of Nazi Germany in the Continuation War (1941–1944), which resulted in the Finnish Air Force's eclectic mix of American, British, French, German and Italian aircraft.

After being defeated in the Battle of Britain, Hitler turned his attention to the Russian bear in the east with its natural resources. He launched Operation *Barbarossa* in the early morning hours of June 22, 1941, invading with four million troops along a 1,800-mile front. It was the largest invasion force in the history of warfare.

Although numerically superior with over 19,000 aircraft, the Soviet Air Force (VVS) was initially technologically inferior, with far less experienced pilots than their Luftwaffe opponents. Stalin's pre-war purges of the VVS created an intellectual deficit as well.

In the first three days, the Luftwaffe claimed over 3,100 Soviet aircraft destroyed, versus the loss of only 78 German aircraft. As incredible as that seems, according to official documents in reality Soviet losses were likely higher. The Luftwaffe quickly achieved localized air supremacy over the battlefields, but could not continue this dominance over the whole expanse of the western Soviet Union.

By mid-July, the Germans had advanced to the outskirts of Kiev in the south, Moscow in the center, and Leningrad in the north. In August 1941, the Germans attacked Leningrad, eventually cutting it off from all land supply routes and starting a siege that lasted for 900 days.

In the south, the Germans captured Kiev in late September, with Soviet losses of nearly half a million men. They then began their drive towards Moscow in late September, although the cold, rainy weather slowed their advance. Extended supply lines strained German logistics, but as the ground hardened due to freezing temperatures, they once again began their march to Moscow. But neither the Wehrmacht nor the Luftwaffe were prepared for the long harsh winter, and the Soviet counterattack in early December pushed them back over 200 miles, effectively ending the Battle for Moscow.

The summer of 1942 saw another large-scale German offensive, specifically aimed at capturing Soviet oil fields. The decisive Soviet victory at Stalingrad (August 1942 to February 1943) was arguably the turning point of World War II.

The final German offensive on the Eastern Front commenced with the Battle of Kursk (July 5 to August 23, 1943), the largest armored battle ever fought, involving over 11,000 tanks, nearly 3.5 million men, and 5,600 supporting aircraft. It was also another decisive Soviet victory, aided by the Allied invasion of Sicily on July 10, which prompted Hitler to redeploy forces from Kursk to Italy.

Combat losses steadily weakened the Luftwaffe's strength on the Eastern Front which was accelerated when fighter squadrons were sent back to defend Germany against the Allied strategic bombing campaign. The Allied bombing also stretched German fuel supplies to their limits.

Now fully mobilized, the Soviet industry developed and manufactured much-improved fighters and ground attack aircraft along with better-trained pilots. The Allied Lend Lease program also helped the Soviets survive by providing over half of their high octane aviation fuel and nearly a third of their aircraft.

By the beginning of the Belorussian Offensive on June 22, 1944, the Soviets achieved a 10:1 advantage in armor and 7:1 in aircraft on the battlefield. By July 1944, they had reached the prewar Polish border.

Entering Warsaw on January 17, 1945, the Soviets rapidly advanced across the Baltic States and eastern Prussia, closing in on Berlin. After weeks of intense house-to-house fighting, Berlin finally surrendered to the Soviets on May 2, 1945.

Some of the largest and most ferocious battles of World War II were fought on the Eastern Front, resulting in half of the deaths of the conflict, many of them civilians. The aftermath of Hitler's gamble against the Russian bear created a political landscape that, for the next 50 years, would divide Europe on two sides of an Iron Curtain.

 Luftwaffe Heinkel He 111s, Soviet Union, 1942. The Luftwaffe had three *Kampfgeschwaders* of He 111s at the start of Operation *Barbarossa* on June 22, 1941. He 111s were primarily used to provide tactical support to the German Army on the Eastern Front, but after suffering heavy losses they were reassigned to a transport role.

 RAF Hawker Hurricane Mk II, Soviet Union, March 8, 1942. An RAF Hurricane test firing its 0.303in machine guns, with one tracer out of every four rounds. The British and Canadians sent almost 3,000 Hurricanes to the Soviet Union from 1941 to 1944. The Soviet pilots were generally disappointed with the fighter because it was slower than the opposition and lacked hard-hitting armament.

 Luftwaffe Heinkel He 111, Kursk, Russia, July 5, 1943. On the first day of the Battle of Kursk, Wilhelm "Willi" Kriessmann on his second mission of the day had his bomber's left engine shot up by Russian Yak-9 fighters. He was able to safely land the bomber back in friendly territory, and the crew escaped. Kriessmann flew his last combat mission two days later but continued as a ferry pilot, eventually delivering new Arado 234 jet bombers from the factories to the front lines.

Soviet AF Yakovlev Yak-9D, Finland, September 2, 1944. A Finnish soldier sits in a Soviet Yak-9 fighter that two Russian officers had crash landed in Lappeenranta, Finland on August 30, 1944. Pilot Lieutenant Mikhail Volkov and Sub Lieutenant Titorenko (who hid in the storage compartment), were believed to have defected in order to warn the Finnish of an upcoming Soviet offensive.

 Luftwaffe Focke-Wulf Fw 190A-6, Immola, Finland, July 2, 1944.
This Fw 190A-6 deployed to Finland as part of Battle Group
Kuhlmey – the temporary Luftwaffe organization assigned from
June 16 to August 12, 1944 to help the Finnish stop the Russian
advance on the Karelian Isthmus (the narrow strip of land
connecting Leningrad, now St Petersburg, and Finland). On the
evening this photograph was taken, the Soviet Air Force launched
a surprise attack on Immola, destroying nine aircraft and damaging
24 more. The next day, Major Erich Rudorffer, commander of
II./JG 54 and history's seventh most successful fighter pilot with
222 victories, shot down five Russian Il-2s within five minutes.

 Soviet AF Polikarpov I-15 Chaika, Russia, date unknown. The
I-15 Chaika (Seagull) saw combat with the Spanish Republicans in
the Spanish Civil War, with the Chinese in the Pacific Theater, and
with the Soviets against Finland during the Winter War (1940). It
also saw limited service against the Germans.

 Luftwaffe Focke-Wulf Fw 190A-4, Krasnogvardeysk, Russia, winter 1942–43. Wearing its winter camouflage scheme, "White 1" assigned to 1 Staffel of Jagdgeschwader 54 "Grunherz" (Green Hearts) lands at Krasnogvardeysk (now called Gatchina), Russia. JG 54 claimed its 4,000th kill on February 23, 1943.

 Soviet Yakovlev Yak-9s and USAAF Boeing B-17s, Poltava Airfield, Russia, summer 1944. USAAF bombers flew seven shuttle bombing missions starting in June 1944. Taking off from their home bases in England and Italy, they bombed targets in Eastern Europe before landing in Russia.

 RAF Hawker Hurricane Mk IIb, Murmansk, Russia, October 1941. This aircraft was assigned to RAF Squadron Leader Tony Rook of No 81 Squadron, 151 Wing, near Murmansk, Russia, and was one of 24 Hurricanes the British sent to Russia onboard the carrier HMS *Argus*, with another 16 in crates. Arriving in September 1941, the wing shot down 14 German aircraft during its three weeks of flying. Squadron Leader Rook shot down a German bomber and shared a Bf 109 kill in this Hurricane (to add to his kill in the Battle of Britain). He was awarded the DFC, as well as the Russian Order of Lenin (one of only four British airmen so honored) for his actions in Russia. By late October 1941 the Hurricanes had been handed over to the Russians.

 Soviet AF Polikarpov I-16, Finland/Russia border, December 10, 1941. The Polikarpov I-16 was the world's first low-wing monoplane fighter with retractable landing gear and was the main Soviet fighter at the beginning of the war.

 Soviet AF Lavochkin La-5, Russia, spring 1943. Although the La-5 suffered from a lack of fuel (only 40 minutes at cruise power), it excelled in air-to-air combat below 10,000ft. The farmers of the Gorky region paid for the construction of this La-5 as part of a squadron named "Eskadrilya Valeriy Chkalov" (the writing on the left side of the fuselage) after famed Soviet test pilot Valeriy Chkalov.

 Finnish AF Messerschmitt Bf 109G, Suulajärvi, Finland, May 12, 1944. The Finnish AF bought 162 Bf 109s and achieved a 25:1 kill ratio against the Soviets with it. On June 17, 1944, Lieutenant Lauria Nissinen (32.5 kill ace) was leading a flight of 10 Bf 109s when a Soviet La-5 shot the wing off 12.5 kill ace Lieutenant Urho Sarjamo's Bf 109 (the aircraft in the picture), and the wreckage hit Nissinen's machine, killing both aces.

 Finnish AF Brewster Buffalo, Finland, winter. The Brewster Buffalo was already obsolete at the beginning of the war. However, the Finnish AF bought 44 of the type and flew them from 1940 to 1944 with great success. In the only aerial engagement between the Finnish Buffalos and the Luftwaffe on October 3, 1944, two Ju 87s were shot down for no losses.

 Finnish AF Brewster Buffalo, Finland, winter. The Finnish AF had 36 Buffalo aces, including the top scoring Finnish ace, Ilmari Juutilainen, who scored 34 of his 94.5 kills in the type. Finnish pilots called their aircraft the "Brewster," or "Taivaan Helmi" (Pearl of the Skies). With over a 25:1 kill ratio, the last Brewster victory over a Soviet aircraft was on June 17, 1944.

 Finnish AF Hawker Hurricane Mk I, Finland, September 14, 1941.
The Finnish bought 12 Hurricane Mk Is from Britain on February 17, 1940. Owing to the limited number of aircraft and spare parts, Hurricanes were of limited use to the Finnish AF.

 Luftwaffe Messerschmitt Bf 109E-7/B, Romania, March 1941.
Leutnant Peter-Paul Steindl of II./JG 54 was an Austrian pilot that transferred to the Luftwaffe in 1938. Credited with 10 victories, he flew this spectacularly camouflaged aircraft. Steindl died during a test flight of a Focke-Wulf Fw 190D-9 on January 9, 1945.

CHAPTER FOUR

WAKING THE GIANT

Should hostilities once break out between Japan and the United States, it would not be enough that we take Guam and the Philippines, nor even Hawaii and San Francisco. To make victory certain, we would have to march into Washington and dictate the terms of peace in the White House. I wonder if our politicians (who speak so lightly of a Japanese-American war) have confidence as to the final outcome and are prepared to make the necessary sacrifices.

Admiral Isoroku Yamamoto, Imperial Japanese Navy, Commander-in-Chief, Combined Fleet

AIR RAID ON PEARL HARBOR X THIS IS NOT DRILL

Rear Admiral Husband E. Kimmel, Commander-in-Chief Pacific (CINCPAC) message, December 7, 1941

Despite the battles raging throughout Europe and the Pacific from 1939 to 1941, the US remained staunchly neutral. The horrors of World War I, the still faltering economy after the Great Depression and the reluctance to get entangled in another foreign war created strong non-interventionist sentiments in the American public.

After the fall of France in 1940, however, the US began to realize that it needed to quickly expand its military and instituted the first peacetime draft. In May 1940, President Franklin D. Roosevelt asked US industry for an unprecedented production program of 50,000 aircraft a year.

The American people slowly grasped that the Axis powers were fundamentally opposed to freedom and democracy. Thus, while still neutral, the US turned into an "Arsenal of Democracy," as laid out in Roosevelt's speech of December 29, 1940. The Lend-Lease Act, signed on March 11, 1941, allowed the US to lease or sell arms to "any country whose defense the President deems vital to the defense of the United States."

Some Americans, however, ached to get into the fight. Several pilots joined the Royal Air Force to fight for Britain (eventually becoming the "Eagle" Squadrons), while others flew for the American Volunteer Group (the "Flying Tigers") in China.

In response to Japan's invasion of French Indochina in 1940, the US halted shipment of aircraft, parts, machine tools, and aviation gasoline to Japan. In early 1941, the US moved its Pacific Fleet from San Diego to Pearl Harbor, Hawaii, and increased its military presence in the Philippines. The US ceased all exports to Japan in July 1941, compelling the Japanese to take the Dutch East Indies for its natural resources.

Tensions escalated further when Roosevelt warned on August 17 that the US was prepared to take steps against Japan if it attacked neighboring countries. The Japanese were then faced with the difficult choice of withdrawing from China and losing face, or seizing new sources of raw materials.

As negotiations continued into the Fall, the Japanese made plans to strike first. They studied the November 11, 1940 British attack on the Italian fleet at Taranto, and modified their torpedoes so they would work in the shallow waters of Pearl Harbor. On November 26 (November 27 in Japan), the final American proposal required Japan to evacuate China. The day before, however, the Japanese fleet had already sailed, bound for Pearl Harbor.

By late 1941, the majority of Americans expected war with Japan. Despite American strategists as far back as the 1920s indicating the possibility of an attack at Pearl Harbor, they still expected the primary attack in the Philippines. The Japanese anticipated that a pre-emptive strike at Pearl Harbor would prevent the US Fleet from interfering with Japanese plans in Southeast Asia, undermine American morale and lead to a negotiated peace.

On a beautiful December 7 Sunday morning at 0748hrs, 353 Japanese fighters, bombers and torpedo bombers from six aircraft carriers attacked the Pacific Fleet and military bases on Oahu, forcefully dragging America into the war. The surprise attack killed 2,403 Americans and wounded another 1,178, sank 18 ships (including five battleships), and destroyed or damaged 347 aircraft. The next day, in his speech asking the US Congress for a declaration of war on Japan, Roosevelt declared that December 7, 1941 would be "a date which will live in infamy." On December 11, Germany and Italy declared war on the US.

With America's entrance into the war, the full might of US industry and innovation became engaged in the fight for freedom. In December 1941, the US Navy had 350 major combatant ships; by the end of the war, it consisted of over 1,200 warships. In 1943 alone, American shipbuilders constructed 15 large and 50 smaller aircraft carriers.

In September 1939, the US Army Air Corps consisted of 20,000 men and 2,400 aircraft, which were inferior to their British, German and Japanese counterparts. By 1944, the Army Air Forces had expanded to 2.4 million personnel and 80,000 aircraft, and American industry produced nearly 100,000 advanced aircraft.

With production like this, the Axis powers had no hope in what was to become a war of attrition against the giant "Arsenal of Democracy."

...we here highly resolve that these dead shall not have died in vain...

REMEMBER DEC. 7th!

USAAF Curtiss P-40, Wheeler Army Airfield, Hawaii, December 7, 1941. Men examine the charred wreckage of a P-40 following the Japanese attack. They have just removed the propeller and are seeing if anything else can be salvaged. One third of the aircraft assigned to Wheeler were destroyed in the raid.

US Navy Consolidated PBY-5 Catalina, NAS Kaneohe, Hawaii, December 7, 1941. Sailors moving a Catalina during the Japanese strike on Hawaii. The first bombs of the attack fell on NAS Kaneohe nine minutes before Pearl Harbor was attacked.

Imperial Japanese Navy Aichi D3A1, Pearl Harbor, Hawaii, December 1941. US Navy sailors recover a "Val" dive bomber belonging to the Japanese carrier *Kaga* that was shot down by the USS *Nevada*. Of the 344 Japanese aircraft that attacked Hawaii, only 29 were lost.

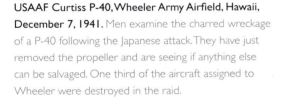

 USAAF Bell P-39C/Ds, Selfridge Field, Michigan, 1941. The P-39C was the first production version of the Airacobra and entered US Army Air Corps service in February 1941 with the 31st Pursuit Group at Selfridge Field. Although the P-39 was not generally viewed as a very effective combat aircraft, many successful American fighter pilots trained on Airacobras prior to going into combat.

 USAAF WASPs, Avenger Field, Texas, date unknown. At the start of the war, America was short of pilots, so the USAAF created the Women Airforce Service Pilots (WASPs) in 1942 to ferry aircraft and relieve male pilots for combat duty. The WASPs flew everything in the USAAF, ranging from trainers to the fastest fighters and biggest bombers.

 US Navy Vought F4U-1, Goodyear Factory, summer 1943.
A new Corsair receiving its coat of paint. The Corsair's bent wings were to accommodate the long propeller without requiring unnecessarily long landing gear.

 USAAF North American A-36A, Louisiana, 1943. USAAF fighter pilots of a training squadron in front of an A-36A Apache, the ground-attack/dive bomber version of the P-51 Mustang. The A-36A had six 0.50in machine guns (two were in the nose), dive-brake, and bomb racks and was the first Mustang variant used in combat by the USAAF.

 USAAF Consolidated B-24D, Fort Worth, Texas, September 28, 1942. President Franklin D. Roosevelt, his wife, daughter-in-law, and Major General Richard Donovan (Eighth Army Corps commander) make a surprise visit to the Consolidated plant. George Newman, the plant manager, shows them around the nation's largest aircraft factory.

 USAAF North American B-25B, USS *Hornet*, April 1942. In the wake of Pearl Harbor, 16 B-25 Mitchell bombers led by Lieutenant Colonel Jimmy Doolittle carried out a surprise attack against Japan. Forced to launch early when their carrier was spotted by a Japanese ship, the bombers did not have enough fuel to reach their intended landing airfields in China. Miraculously, all but three of the 80 crew members survived the raid.

 USAAF North American AT-6, Harlingen, Texas, date unknown. Over 48,000 students were trained in the art of aerial gunnery at the Harlingen Aerial Gunnery School between December 1941 and October 1, 1945. Here, the student is in the backseat of an AT-6 Texan trainer.

 USAAF Lockheed P-38F, Burbank, California, July 1942. Starting in April 1942, Lockheed began producing the P-38F, which gave the Lightning the ability to carry fuel tanks or bombs under the wings inboard of the engines. Of the 10,037 Lightnings produced, Lockheed built some 527 P-38Fs.

 USAAF North American B-25H and P-51Bs, Inglewood, California, July 1943. The B-25 in the foreground was the first production B-25H (of 1,000), featuring a 75mm cannon and four 0.50in machine guns in the nose. The left P-51B nearest the camera went down in Hungary on July 2, 1944. Flown by Major Stephen Andrew, a nine-victory ace of the 486th Fighter Squadron, 352nd Fighter Group, he lost his engine over Budapest while escorting bombers from Italy on one of the shuttle missions. He was captured and became a prisoner of war.

 USAAF Major Robert S. Johnson, Long Island, New York, June 1944. Major Robert S. Johnson scored 27 kills while flying P-47s with the 56th Fighter Group over Europe. Ordered home for a War Bond tour, he was applauded by thousands of workers at the Republic plant at Farmingdale, Long Island, where the P-47 Thunderbolt was produced.

 USAAF B-17, Long Beach, California, October 1942. The female worker at the Douglas Aircraft Factory is finishing the Plexiglas nose of a B-17F bomber, designed by Boeing. Of the 12,731 B-17s produced during the war, Douglas built 3,000.

 USAAF Lockheed P-38J, Burbank, California, 1944. The P-38 Lightning was the only American fighter in production throughout the American involvement in the war (1941–45), and shot down more Japanese aircraft than any other USAAF type.

CHAPTER FIVE

WAR IN THE MED

Everything was affected by sand – it got everywhere. Into your hair, clothing and eyes, between teeth, into your food and drink, and unfortunately, into every bit of moving machinery, where it displayed a depressingly abrasive effect.

Group Captain Billy Drake, RAF, 23.5-kill ace

I took along a lot of bad habits with me which I acquired in Russia. In Africa, you just couldn't get away with that sort of thing. The RAF promptly shot me down and in the process snapped me back to the realities of war in the air.

General Johannes "Macky" Steinhoff, Luftwaffe, 176-kill ace

In the 1930s, dictator Benito Mussolini planned an Italian expansion across the Mediterranean and North Africa. On October 2, 1935, he launched an invasion of Abyssinia (present-day Ethiopia), and on April 7, 1939, he invaded Albania, occupying the country in only two days. The next month, Italy formally allied with Nazi Germany.

To counter these moves, Britain sent reinforcements to Egypt. Italy declared war on France and the United Kingdom on June 10, 1940 and the siege of Malta began the next day with the first Italian air attacks. Only 60 miles from Sicily, Malta was a threat to Italian dominance of the Mediterranean. Initially, Malta's air defense consisted of six obsolete Gladiator biplanes, but they were soon reinforced by Hurricanes (and Spitfires in early 1942). One of the most intensively bombed areas of the war, Malta's successful defense gave the Allies a base of operations to attack Axis supply lines, which eventually caused fuel shortages in Libya.

Meanwhile, Italian ground forces invaded Egypt on September 13, 1940, and on October 28 they invaded Greece.

On the night of November 12–13, 1940, the Royal Navy, flying Swordfish biplane torpedo bombers, attacked the Italian fleet at anchor in Taranto harbor. The Italian fleet lost half of its big ships in one night, but control of the Mediterranean would swing back and forth until the Italian armistice in 1943.

In the spring of 1941, Axis forces under General Erwin Rommel forced a British retreat in North Africa and surrounded the garrison at Tobruk for 241 days. Meanwhile, British forces arrived in Greece in March 1941, and German troops moved into Bulgaria. In April, German, Italian, Hungarian and Bulgarian forces captured Yugoslavia in 11 days, triggering an uprising of communist guerrillas led by Josip Tito.

The Germans came to the aid of the Italians and invaded Greece on April 6, 1941, causing the Greek surrender by the end of the month. British forces retreated to the island of Crete, where the Germans launched an airborne invasion on May 20, capturing the island by June 1. Having secured their southern flank, the Germans then turned their attention eastwards to the Soviet Union.

Later in 1941, British counterattacks in North Africa forced an Axis retreat back to where they began the year. In 1942, Axis forces once again drove the British back, this time capturing Tobruk. The British retreated all the way to El Alamein (in Egypt), where the British Eighth Army decisively defeated the Axis at the Second Battle of El Alamein (October 23 to November 11, 1942). Winston Churchill said after the war: "Before Alamein we never had a victory. After Alamein we never had a defeat."

Simultaneously, on November 8, Allied forces landed in Algeria and Morocco. During the invasion, negotiations with French Admiral Francois Darlan (the commander of French forces) took place, and he ordered all French troops in North Africa to cease resistance and instead co-operate with the Allies. In response, Hitler ordered the occupation of Vichy France.

Now fighting on two fronts, with the British Eighth Army approaching from the east and the British, Free French, and American forces from the west, the Italian-German forces in North Africa surrendered in Tunisia on May 13, 1943.

The Allies invaded Sicily on July 10, 1943, and on July 25 the Italian government deposed Mussolini. This led Hitler to redeploy forces from the Eastern Front during the Battle of Kursk to defend Italy. The Allies entered Messina on August 17 as the last vestiges of the German troops evacuated.

The British invaded the "toe" of Italy on September 3, and the new Italian government surrendered that same day. The next week American and British forces landed at Salerno, and British airborne troops landed at Taranto.

However, the Italian terrain proved ideal for the German defense, and the Allies slogged up the Italian boot. An amphibious invasion at Anzio on January 22, 1944 was intended to outflank the German defensive lines and open a path to Rome, but the American commanders failed to quickly capitalize on the initial successes. Eventually, a frontal assault at Monte Cassino broke through and the Allies captured Rome on June 4, 1944 – the first Axis capital to fall.

Fighting continued up the Italian peninsula until the German armed forces in Italy eventually surrendered on May 2, 1945.

 USAAF North American B-25, Mediterranean, date unknown.
B-25s of the 12th Air Force on their way to bomb a railroad in
northern Italy.

 USAAF North American B-25C, North Africa, spring 1943.
The "Desert Warrior," a B-25 Mitchell of the 81st Bomb
Squadron, 12th Bomb Group, and its crew about to be sent
back to the US after completing 73 combat missions in the
Mediterranean Theater.

 Italian AF Breda Ba.65, North Africa, date unknown.
A British soldier inspects the burnt-out wreckage of an
Italian Ba.65 ground-attack aircraft. About 150 Ba.65s
were still in service when Italy entered the war in June
1940, but most were shot down or withdrawn by
February 1941.

 USAAF Lockheed P-38G, Algeria, May 1943. After successfully completing a fighter bomber
mission, 1st Lieutenant John MacKay, 2nd Lieutenant Samuel Sweet, 2nd Lieutenant Warren
Holden, and 2nd Lieutenant Frank McIntosh of the 27th Fighter Squadron, 1st Fighter Group were
headed home when they were jumped by over 20 German fighters. The ensuing dogfight lasted
25 minutes, an eternity in air-to-air combat. The pilots were credited with two kills each, and added
to MacKay's three victories from April 5, 1943, making him an ace. "Shoot..You're Faded" was
MacKay's aircraft.

USAAF Republic P-47D, Italy, February 1945. P-47s of the 346th Fighter Squadron, 350th Fighter Group, carrying external fuel tanks on a bomber escort mission near the Austrian border. 1st Lieutenant Homer J. St. Onge is flying the closest aircraft ("Torrid Tess," also named "Philadelphia Filly" on the right side). He was in this aircraft on a strafing mission on April 27, 1945, when he was hit by anti-aircraft fire but safely belly-landed near Ghedi, Italy. Partisans returned him to friendly lines.

 BEF Republic P-47, Italy, 1945. As part of the Brazilian Expeditionary Force (BEF), 48 fighter pilots and their support personnel were sent to Europe to fight alongside the USAAF in Italy. The 1st Brazilian Fighter Squadron was initially assigned to the 350th Fighter Group and flew 2,550 sorties between November 11, 1944 and May 2, 1945. The squadron destroyed hundreds of vehicles and barges on April 22, a date now commemorated as "Brazilian Fighter Arm Day."

 RAF Bristol Beaufighter Mk VIF, Sicily, August 1943. No 600 Squadron Beaufighters in their dispersals amongst the olive trees at Cassibile Airfield, Sicily. Second from right is Wing Commander Charles "Paddy" Green, commanding officer of the highest scoring night fighter squadron in the RAF. Credited with a total of 11 kills, Green scored seven of his victories over three consecutive nights in July 1943 over Sicily, including downing four Ju 88s in one mission.

 Italy, 1944. Famous Hollywood actress Marlene Dietrich in the chow line with members of the 47th Bomb Group.

 USAAF Lockheed P-38L, Italy, November 1944.
A four-ship of P-38Ls from the 1st Fighter Group. Aircraft "13" (the second closest to the camera) was involved in a landing accident in California on August 2, 1945.

 RAF Martin Baltimore, North Africa, date unknown.
Although built by the Glenn L. Martin Company in the US, the Baltimore was not used by US forces. Instead, it became a versatile light attack bomber with the Commonwealth, Greek, and Italian Co-Belligerent Air Forces.

 Italian AF CANT Z1007bis, North Africa, date unknown. The CANT Z1007 Alcione (Kingfisher) was an Italian medium bomber and torpedo bomber with a wooden structure and a crew of five. The wood was subject to cracks and delamination in the harsh climates of North Africa and Russia.

 Italian AF Fiat CR.42, Ciampino, Italy, spring 1942. An ace with three kills in the Spanish Civil War and another two victories in East Africa in 1940–41 over RAF Blenheims, Captain Corrado Ricci starts his aircraft for another night mission. Flying CR.42CNs (modified for night operations), Ricci commanded the *Regia Aeronautica*'s 300th Squadron from January to May 1942 in the night defense of Rome. After the Italian Armistice in September 1943, Ricci served with the Italian Co-Belligerent Air Force.

 **Luftwaffe Junkers Ju 87, Libya, January 1942.** The Kittyhawk Ia (P-40E) saw combat for the first time in North Africa on January 1, 1942, when nine aircraft from No 3 Squadron RAF attacked a German formation of 16 Ju 87 Stukas being escorted by six Bf 109s. The British pilots shot down four Stukas (one of which is being studied here by a British officer) and one Bf 109.

USAAF Consolidated B-24H, Austria, August 23, 1944. The horror of the air-to-air war. B-24 "Extra Joker" of the 725th Bomb Squadron, 451st Bomb Group, took off from Castellucio Airfield, Italy, on a daylight bombing raid against Markersdorf Airdrome, near Vienna, Austria. En route, it was badly shot up by Luftwaffe Focke-Wulf Fw 190s. Although the fire behind the number one (left outboard) engine seems small, it quickly reached the fuel tank. The aircraft burst into flames and went out of control. All 10 members of 1st Lt Kenneth Whiting's crew were killed.

 USAAF North American B-25D, Italy, March 1944.
On their way to bomb German targets in northern Italy,
B-25s of the 447th Bomb Squadron, 321st Bomb Group,
fly past Mt. Vesuvius as it spews ash.

 USAAF North American B-25, Italy, March 1944. Stationed
at Pompeii, 78 to 88 B-25s of the 340th Bomb Group were
destroyed during the March 18–23, 1944, eruption of Mt. Vesuvius.

 Italian AF Reggiane Re.2002, Italy, July 1943. These Reggiane Re.2002 Arietes (Rams) of 239th Squadron, 102nd Group, are leaving Tarquinia (north of Rome) for southern Italy to counter the Allied invasion of Sicily. The first mission on July 10 saw three of eight Re.2002s shot down while attacking Allied ships, including the group commander. They continued to suffer heavy losses until the Italian surrender in September 1943. After the Armistice, the Luftwaffe used Re.2002s to attack the French resistance, while the Italian Co-Belligerent Air Force flew them alongside the Allies.

 RAF Short Stirling, Italy, October 11, 1944. The Stirling entered the RAF as a heavy bomber in early 1941, but was soon replaced by more advanced aircraft. Although pleasant to fly once airborne, the Stirling was difficult to take off in and land and had disappointing performance at altitude. By late 1943, Stirlings were being withdrawn from service as bombers and used instead for minelaying and glider towing. USAAF P-38s and P-47s are in the background.

 RAF Curtiss Tomahawk IIB, North Africa, September 1941. Noted for its shark mouth nose art, No 112 Squadron flew the Tomahawk IIB (an export version of the P-40C) from July to December 1941. Aircraft "A" was delivered to the squadron on June 15, 1941, and Sergeant Frederick D. Glasgow (RNZAF) lost his life over Libya in it when he was shot down by a Bf 109 on November 25, 1941.

 RAF Spitfire Mk VIII, Italy, date unknown. USAAF aircrew, including an African-American pilot of the Tuskegee Airmen, hitch a ride on a jeep next to a British Spitfire. Tuskegee Airmen was the popular name for African-American pilots who flew as part of the 332nd Fighter Group and 477th Bomb Group.

 Italian AF Macchi C.202, location and date unknown.
The Macchi C.202 Folgore (Thunderbolt) was a development
of the C.200 with a license-built version of the Bf 109 engine.
After the Armistice, C.202s served with both the Italian
Co-Belligerent Air Force and the *Aeronautica Nazionale*
Repubblicana (on the Axis side).

 USAAF Martin B-26Cs, Germany, February 25, 1945. B-26 Marauders of the 95th Bomb
Squadron, 17th Bomb Group, fly past a column of smoke rising from a German ammunition
storage site and suspected V-2 rocket site near Siegelsbach, southeast of Heidelberg, Germany.
Aircrew who returned from the mission reported debris from the explosions hit their aircraft
as they passed over the target.

 RAF Supermarine Spitfire Mk Vb, Algeria, North Africa, 1943.
Parked in their dispersals in Algeria, these No 154 Squadron
Spitfire Mk Vbs are being readied for their next sortie. In their first
two weeks on operations in North Africa in November 1942,
No 154 Squadron claimed 19 Luftwaffe bombers shot down.
On November 28, Flying Officer "Paddy" Chambers spotted a flight
of five S.79s bombing an Allied convoy. After he shot down four
of them, his wingman Flying Officer Alan Aikman shot down the
remaining bomber.

 Italian AF Savoia-Marchetti S.79, Italy, date unknown. The S.79
Sparviero (Sparrowhawk) was designed as a fast passenger aircraft
in the late 1930s and set 26 world speed records. First seeing
action in the Spanish Civil War, it achieved success in World War II
as a torpedo bomber in the Mediterranean. It was the most
numerous Italian bomber of the war, with around 1,300 built.

 USAAF Curtiss P-40F, USS *Ranger*, January 19, 1943. After 11 days onboard ship, Lieutenant Colonel Gordon Austin prepares to take off for Cazes Aerodrome near Casablanca. Austin served as the 325th Fighter Group commander from December 1942 – July 1943 (achieving two air-to-air kills). To aid in visual identification for the invasion of North Africa, the aircraft initially carried the American flag on the fuselage in front of the insignia.

 Luftwaffe Bf 109E-7/Tropical, Sicily, April 1941. Pilots of 1./JG 27 brief for the final leg of their transfer to Ain-El-Gazala, Libya. Arriving on April 18, 1./JG 27 claimed their first victories in North Africa the next day. One of the claims was by Staffelkapitän (squadron commander) Oberleutnant Karl-Wolfgang Redlich (holding papers on the left), flying "White 1" (in the middle background). Redlich scored 45 victories but was shot down and killed in action on May 29, 1944, while intercepting a group of bombers over Austria.

 Grottaglie Airfield, Fall 1940. When Italy declared war on Britain and France on June 10, 1940, the 2nd Gruppo of 6 Stormo (Fighter Wing) was equipped with a mixture of Fiat CR.32 and CR.42 biplanes and Fiat G.50s. The 2nd Gruppo soon began operations in the Mediterranean and North Africa. Lieutenant Giacomo Metellini stands in front of the 6 Stormo building with its Red Devils insignia.

 Italian AF Macchi C.200, Sicily, 1940. A C.200 Saetta (Arrow) fighter pilot of the 81st Squadron based at Catania-Fontanarossa, Sicily, has to leave his friend behind on this sortie. The C.200s on Sicily were the first to see combat when on June 23, 1940, a C.200 escorting bombers was shot down by an RAF Gladiator.

USAAF Lockheed F-5A, North Africa, late 1943. The F-5A of the 90th Photo Reconnaissance Wing was based on the P-38G Lightning, except that it replaced the machine guns and cannon with high-powered cameras.

 USN Grumman F4F-4, USS *Ranger*, November 1942. A Wildcat of VF-41 "Red Rippers" about to launch against Vichy French airfields near Casablanca. From November 8–10, the pilots of VF-41 claimed 14 Vichy French aircraft shot down for the loss of seven of its own. Circling above are two Army Piper L-4 Cub observation planes that had also launched from the carrier and are about to fly to the invasion beaches.

 USAAF Boeing B-17F, Algeria, 1943. Mechanics change the engine on "The Reluctant Dragon," a B-17F which flew with the 97th, 99th, 301st and 483rd Bomb Groups.

 USAAF North American P-51C, Ramitelli, Italy, August 8, 1944. Captain Andrew "Jug" Turner, commander of the 100th Fighter Squadron, 332nd Fighter Group, signals as he is about to start the engine of his P-51C "Skipper's Darlin' III." Turner took command of the 100th Fighter Squadron in June 1944 and flew 69 combat missions. He was killed on September 14, 1947, in a mid-air collision.

Pilot - Capt. A. Turner.
C/Chief - S/Sgt. U. Cochran.
Asst - Sgt. C. Bentley.
C/Arm - Cpl. H. Beguesse.

 USAAF North American B-25J, Mediterranean, 1944. A B-25 Mitchell of the 12th Bomb Group with "Finito Benito, Next Hirohito" written across its wings. The 12th Bomb Group left the Mediterranean in the early spring of 1944 to fight the Japanese from bases in India.

 Various, Italy, October 1944. Numerous Allied aircraft can be seen on this busy airfield, including an RAF Dakota and USAAF C-47 in the foreground. Behind are B-24s and B-17s, as well as a Savoia-Marchetti S.79 (being fueled). In addition, RAF Handley-Page Halifax heavy bombers (with black fuselages in the middle of the picture) and Vickers Warwick bombers (white aircraft in the background on the right) are also featured.

CHAPTER SIX

CBI THEATER

War came to Japan in June of 1944. The effect on our population was unmistakable. On June 15 the people of Japan were shocked to hear that twenty [B-29] bombers, tremendous giants of the air which dwarfed the powerful B-17, had flown an incredible distance from China to attack a city in Northern Kyushu. The raid did little damage, and twenty planes were hardly enough to cause national excitement. But in the homes and the stores, in the factories and on the streets, everywhere in Japan, the people talked about the raid, discussed the fact that our fighters had failed to stop the bombers. They all asked the same questions. Who was next? When? And how many bombers would come?

Sub-Lieutenant Saburo Sakai, Imperial Japanese Navy, 64-kill ace

We had to fly two Hump missions to ferry enough fuel and bombs to fly a single combat mission. We took off from China with about 1,000 gallons of fuel and burned most of that getting to India. Then we loaded almost 4,000 gallons of fuel and used 1,000 gallons to fly back to China. After offloading about 2,000 gallons, we'd go back to India and do it again.

1st Lieutenant Walt Kaestner, USAAF, B-24 pilot, 308th Heavy Bomb Group, Kunming, China

The China-Burma-India (CBI) Theater had a low priority among the Allied nations in World War II. Its immense size, difficult terrain and weather, and complex political landscape, compounded by the "Germany first" doctrine, diminished its importance. Nonetheless, war in the CBI was ferocious – the majority of civilian and military deaths in the Pacific War occurred in the fight between Japan and China.

Conversely, the US viewed the CBI Theater as a way to tie-up large numbers of Japanese troops, as well as a location for airbases from which to strike Japan. Meanwhile Burma and India were part of the British Empire before World War II, and the colonies were aching for independence.

Japan invaded Manchuria in 1931, and captured Beijing in July 1937, followed by Shanghai in November. The Nanking Massacre (or Rape of Nanking) in late 1937 and early 1938 helped sway US public opinion against Japan.

In order to block Allied supplies to China, Japan invaded the northern part of French Indochina (present-day Vietnam, Laos, and Cambodia) in September 1940. On July 21, 1941, Japan occupied the southern part of French Indochina, and from their newly-acquired airbases, Japanese aircraft attacked Malaya, Singapore and the Dutch East Indies.

In mid-1941, the US government financed the American Volunteer Group (AVG), better known as the "Flying Tigers," to help China defend against the Japanese.

The Burma Road linked the port of Rangoon, Burma, with southwest China. The vital port of Rangoon was initially defended successfully by a small RAF detachment and a squadron of the "Flying Tigers." When the main Japanese assault began on January 22, 1942, the British, Burmese and Indian troops held out until forced to evacuate Rangoon on March 7, 1942. As they left, they instituted a "scorched earth" policy, destroying the port and oil terminal facilities to deny the Japanese their use. By late May, the monsoons stopped the Japanese advance that the Allied armies could not.

The British forces were directed to recapture Burma and to reopen land routes with China as their primary goal in the war against Japan. Due to lack of resources, unrest in India, and long supply routes, Britain initially had difficulty launching an effective campaign in Burma. The Japanese invasion of India in the spring/summer of 1944 pushed the Japanese to the limit of their endurance and supplies, as their troops began to starve and the monsoons brought on disease. As the Allied forces pushed them back, it was the greatest defeat of Japan's army to date, with 50–60,000 dead and another 100,000 casualties – most the result of disease, malnutrition, and exhaustion. The British-led assault recaptured Rangoon in May 1945, just as the monsoon rains began once again.

During the years that Japan occupied Burma, the only Allied supply line to the Chinese was an air route operating from airfields in India over the eastern end of the Himalayas, known as "the Hump." The first such mission was flown on April 8, 1942, when DC-3s ferried fuel intended to resupply the Doolittle Raiders. Flying over mountains up to 16,000ft high, the transport aircraft landed at Kunming, China, an airfield 6,200ft above sea level. Initially using DC-3s and C-47s, the Army Air Forces began receiving C-46s in India in April 1943. In addition, C-54s, C-87s, and C-109s were used to fly supplies and B-24s and even B-29s were used as fuel transports. With a lack of reliable maps, few navigation aids, and very little weather information, Allied pilots continued this challenging mission until August 1945.

To attack Japan, the USAAF XX Bomber Command and its B-29 Superfortress bombers began flying missions from Chinese airbases on June 5, 1944. Ten days later, they dropped the first bombs on the Japanese home islands since the Doolittle Raid of 1942. For every B-29 combat mission, they flew an average of six B-29 round-trip supply missions over "the Hump." They continued to fly missions against Japan, China, Indochina and Burma until they joined the growing B-29 fleet in the Marianas in March 1945.

 USAAF Curtiss C-46, Agra, India, date unknown.
A Curtiss C-46 Commando flies low over India's most
famous landmark, the Taj Mahal.

 AVG Curtiss P-40B, China, 1942. The American Volunteer
Group (AVG), known as the "Flying Tigers," was operational from
December 20, 1941 to July 4, 1942 and credited with destroying
297 Japanese aircraft. Pilots of the 3rd Pursuit Squadron, the
"Hell's Angels," pose in front of their squadron leader's Tomahawk.

 USAAF Curtiss C-46, Chabua Airfield, India, November 23, 1944. A C-46 Commando takes off for another cargo mission over "the Hump." Chabua Airfield was one of the largest bases used by USAAF Air Transport Command to fly personnel and cargo across the Himalayas into Burma.

 USAAF North American P-51A Mustangs, Chin Hills, Burma, date unknown. Flown by Major Robert Petit, "Mrs. Virginia" was a P-51A Mustang of the 1st Air Commando Group.

 USAAF Boeing B-29, India, 1944. Nicknamed "Gone with the Wind," this B-29 was the first Superfortress to arrive in the CBI Theater at Chakulia, India, on April 2, 1944. Assigned to the 25th Bomb Squadron, 40th Bomb Group, this aircraft was mistakenly shot down by a British Beaufighter on December 20, 1944, with the navigator, 1st Lieutenant David Lustig, killed.

 USAAF Lockheed F-5B, India, date unknown. Sergeant Miller directs the pilot of "Miss Virginia E," an F-5B of the 9th Photographic Reconnaissance Squadron, out of its revetment for its next mission. The F-5B was the photo reconnaissance version of the P-38J, with only 200 built. On May 11, 1944, 2nd Lieutenant Walter Thompson crashed "Miss Virginia E" at Chittagong, India. He was uninjured but the aircraft was destroyed.

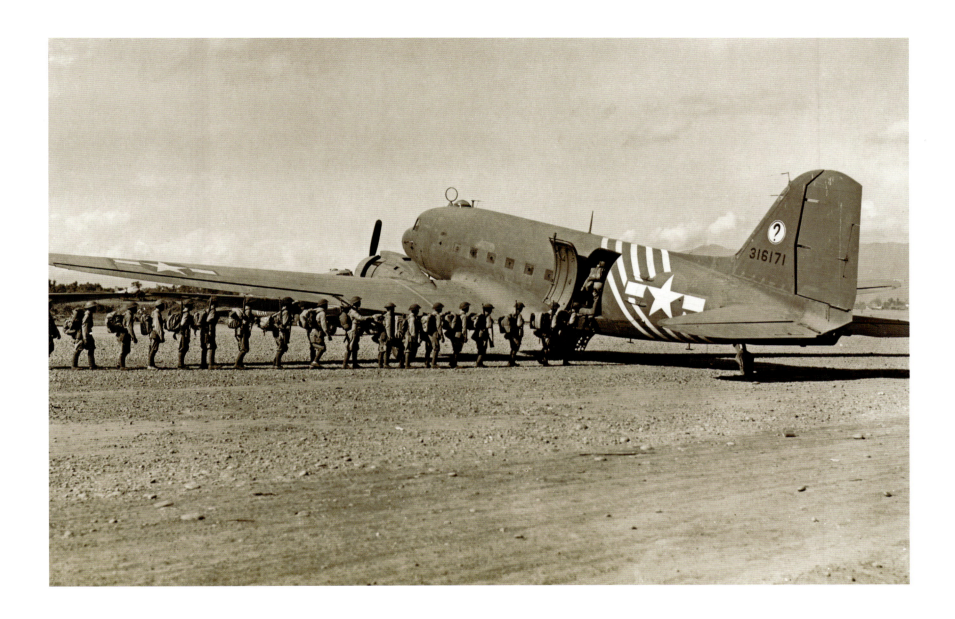

 Hailakandi, India, March 1944. British Major General Orde Charles Wingate discusses plans for an upcoming operation with USAAF Colonel Philip Cochran of the 1st Air Commando Force. Wingate created a long-range penetration unit known as the Chindits. On March 5, 1944, Douglas C-47 Dakota transports and Waco CG-4 gliders began ferrying 9,000 Chindits behind Japanese lines into Burma. Wingate died in an aircraft crash on March 24, 1944.

 USAAF Douglas C-47, Burma, December 10, 1944. Fully loaded Chinese soldiers board their C-47 Dakota transport of the 1st Air Commando Group to be flown into China.

CHAPTER SEVEN

LIBERATING EUROPE

[We] learned that of the 140 pilots, co-pilots, navigators, and bombardiers who had flown across the Atlantic to England on May 31 [1943], just four months and ten days before, we were the only three left on flying status... In the last week, the 100th had lost twenty-one aircraft. In that one week, over 200 men were MIA or KIA.

Captain Harry Crosby, USAAF, Lead Navigator, 100th Bomb Group

We had just crossed the Elbe north of Magdeburg when we first caught sight of the enemy. We let the American formation pass at a respectful distance... Eight hundred bombers went by, 2,000 tons of death, destruction and fire inside their silver bodies, flying to their appointed targets in the heart of Germany. Something had to be done. Wave upon wave, endless formations of four-engined bombers! Right and left above them, with and without vapor trails, a vast pack of Mustang fighters.

Generalleutnant Adolf Galland, Luftwaffe, spring 1944

After two and a half years of conflict, the Allies debated throughout 1942 on the appropriate overall strategy to win the war. Defeating Germany was the primary objective, but there were different approaches. The Soviets demanded an immediate second front to take pressure off of them. The British believed that attacking through the "soft underbelly" of Europe, the peripheral countries like Greece and the Balkans, would be the best way to wear down the German strength and to help shape a postwar Europe. The Americans favored an attack on Germany through France.

While building up strength for such an undertaking, the British and American Allies launched a strategic bombing campaign against Germany. The main aims of the Combined Bomber Offensive were to destroy German industry and morale. RAF bombers attacked Cologne, Germany, on May 30, 1942 in the first "Thousand Bomber" raid. The first American daylight heavy bomber raid over European soil took place on August 17, 1942, signaling the start of an intense aerial war for the skies over Europe. Prior to the Normandy invasion, strategic bombing was the Western Allies' primary effort in Western Europe.

Simultaneously, the Battle of the Atlantic was going on, with German U-boats and Luftwaffe long-range aircraft attacking supply convoys from America to Britain. By April 1943, the U-boats were so successful that supplies in Britain, especially fuel, became critical.

June 6, 1944, forever known as D-Day, was the invasion of northern France against Hitler's "Atlantic Wall." Nearly 160,000 troops crossed the English Channel into France on D-Day, and by the end of August, more than two million Allied troops were on the continent.

Although bogged down in the hedgerows for much longer than anticipated, the Allied armies eventually broke out of Normandy in July and August. In August 1944, the German Army was surrounded by the Western Allies at the Battle of the Falaise Gap. Most of Army Group B was destroyed, with up to 15,000 Germans killed and another 50,000 captured, opening the way to Paris and the German border.

The Allies liberated Paris on August 25, 1944, but the Allied supply lines were quickly getting stretched to the limit. By late August, the US First and Third Armies reported less than a day's supply of fuel on hand, forcing offensive operations to slow to a crawl. As supplies built up again, the Allied forces from Normandy were able to link up with those that had invaded southern France.

The Allies then developed an ambitious plan intended to create an opening into Germany through the Netherlands, as well as capture German V-2 launch sites. Operation "Market Garden," a combined airborne and armor offensive, was fought from September 17–25, 1944.

It quickly turned into an Allied defeat, however, and created a stalemate for the next few months. Constrained by supplies once again, the Allies slowed their advance to the German border.

On December 16, 1944, Germany launched a surprise assault on the Western Front by using most of its remaining reserves in a massive counter-offensive through the Ardennes Forest. Trying to split the Allied forces and capture the port at Antwerp, the Battle of the Bulge showed the Germans were not yet defeated. Low clouds, fog, and winter storms grounded the Allied air forces for several days, allowing the Germans to surround the US 101st Airborne Division in Bastogne. In a massive air raid against Allied airfields on New Year's Day 1945, the Luftwaffe destroyed 465 Allied aircraft, but lost many of its remaining experienced pilots.

As the weather cleared, however, Allied armies and air forces pounded the German forces, which were running low on fuel, back into Germany. In February 1945, the Allied ground forces finally entered Germany from the west, and by March, they crossed the Rhine River. Sweeping rapidly across Germany, the American forces met the Soviets on the Elbe River on April 25. Five days later, Hitler committed suicide. Germany agreed to total and unconditional surrender on May 7 and May 8, 1945 became V-E (Victory in Europe) Day. After almost six years of war, peace finally returned to the European continent.

USAAF Republic P-47D, Liverpool, England, November 19, 1943. After being shipped to England, a Republic P-47 Thunderbolt is trucked from the docks in Liverpool to an airbase to be reassembled and used in the air war over Europe.

USAAF Consolidated B-24D, Alconbury, England, November 9, 1942. "Flying Cock" of the 409th Bomb Squadron, 93rd Bomb Group and its jubilant crew after a mission against the U-boat base at Saint Nazaire, France. "Flying Cock" was badly damaged in a crash landing in early 1943, but was repaired and transferred to North Africa and flew (as "Doodlebug") on the infamous low-level raid against the Ploesti oil refinery on August 1, 1943.

RAF Douglas Havoc, location and date unknown. While the bombardier settles in, a pilot gets into his Havoc for another night intruder mission over occupied Europe. Living up to their name, Havocs caused considerable damage to German targets.

USAAF Martin B-26B, RAF Andrewsfield, England, August 1943. The 'friendly invasion' by the Americans during the war created the largest construction program ever seen in Britain, with many airfields built right alongside farmers' fields. Here, workers are gathering hay as the B-26 Marauder named "Bag O Bolts" of the 450th Bomb Squadron, 322nd Bomb Group, is refueled.

USAAF, France, 1945. Major Ralph Jenkins, commander of the 510th Fighter Squadron, 405th Fighter Group, points to his unit's special qualifications. "Jenkins' Jerry Junkers" flew initially from England, then followed Patton's Third Army all the way through Europe. Credited with two kills, Jenkins flew 129 missions in his P-47 named "Tallahassee Lassie" after his wife. He said, "The love affair between a pilot and his Thunderbolt was irresistible."

RAF Avro Lancaster, location and date unknown. The Lancaster was the main RAF bomber used in the night bombing campaigns over Europe. Its large unobstructed bomb bay meant that it could carry the 12,000lb "Tallboy" and 22,000lb "Grand Slam" earthquake bombs. No 617 Squadron famously flew Lancasters on the Dam Busters raid in May 1943.

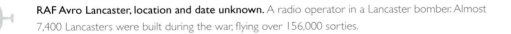
RAF Avro Lancaster, location and date unknown. A radio operator in a Lancaster bomber. Almost 7,400 Lancasters were built during the war, flying over 156,000 sorties.

RAF Handley Page Halifax B.II, Linton-on-Ouse, England, April 3, 1943. Armorers load bombs on a No 76 Squadron Halifax. One of the three heavy bomber types used by the RAF, the Halifax entered service in November 1940. At its peak it was flown by 34 Bomber Command squadrons in Europe. Of the 6,176 built, 1,833 were lost on operations.

 USAAF North American P-51B, Leiston, England, 1944. Captain Clarence "Bud" Anderson in his Mustang of the 363rd Fighter Squadron, 357th Fighter Group. Anderson was promoted to major at the age of 22 and scored 16-and-a-quarter kills in Mustangs he named "Old Crow."

 USAAF North American P-51B, England, August 1944. Originally named "Man O' War" by Lieutenant Colonel Claiborn Kinnard Jr, this Mustang was next assigned to Lieutenant Robert Hulderman who named it "The Iowa Beaut." Hulderman only had one kill but the aircraft still carried Kinnard's 10-kill markings. On September 11, 1944, Captain Kevin Rafferty was lost in "The Iowa Beaut" near Marburg, Germany.

 USAAF Consolidated B-24D, Shipdham, England, date unknown.
A Liberator of the 44th Bomb Group, known as the
"Flying Eight-Balls." Primarily based at Shipdham, with several
detachments to North Africa in 1943, the "Flying Eight-Balls" flew
343 combat missions and lost 153 aircraft during the war.

 **USAAF Boeing B-17G, Great Ashfield, England, 1944.** A rare color
photograph of the bomber named after Corporal Ruby Newell,
voted as the most beautiful woman in the Women's Army Corps
in England.

USAAF North American P-51D, Fowlmere, England, 1944.
Corporal Ruby Newell, voted "Prettiest WAC in England," is
surrounded by admirers as she poses in front of a Mustang
named in her honor. "Miss ETO" was written off in a take-off
accident on March 22, 1945. The pilot to her right, Lieutenant
George Jones Jr, was killed in action on March 3, 1945, when
he was shot down by anti-aircraft fire.

 RAF de Havilland Mosquito, England, date unknown. The crew of a Mosquito about to fly another mission. Constructed almost entirely of wood, the Mosquito was initially developed as a fast bomber but went on to serve successfully as a fighter-bomber, night fighter and photo-reconnaissance aircraft.

 RAF de Havilland Mosquito B.IVs, RAF Marham, England, December 11, 1942. No 105 Squadron was the first unit equipped with the Mosquito, and this image shows the cost of war. The closest aircraft (GB-A) was shot down over the Netherlands on December 22, 1942, killing Flight Sergeant Joseph Cloutier and Sergeant Albert Foxley. GB-E and its crew were lost over France on June 9, 1944, while GB-P crashed on landing on January 27, 1943. GB-J and its crew were lost near Berlin on January 30, 1943 and GB-K was damaged after only two sorties on December 20, 1942.

 USAAF North American P-51D, Fowlmere, England, April 1, 1945. Protestant Easter morning service beside Lieutenant Colonel William Clark's Mustang "Happy IV"/"Dotty" of the 504th Fighter Squadron, 339th Fighter Group. Clark took command of the 339th FG on April 14, 1945. He destroyed eight German aircraft on the ground (six on one mission on April 16, 1945) and shot down one enemy aircraft in this Mustang.

 USAAF Republic P-47D, Duxford, England, May 1944. Staff Sergeants Jim Sterner and Joe McCarthy carry newly-painted engine cowling panels for their checkerboard P-47 Thunderbolt of 83rd Fighter Squadron, 78th Fighter Group.

 RAF Supermarine Spitfire Mk IX, Tangmere, England, July 1944. Norwegian pilot Nils Magne Jørgensen of No 332 (Norwegian) Squadron RAF, waits while the "package" for his return trip to Normandy is prepared. Several British breweries offered free beer to the troops in France after the Normandy landings, so RAF pilots came up with the idea of flying kegs attached to the bomb racks of their aircraft. Soon, long-range fuel tanks were modified to carry the beer, as seen here.

 RAF Avro Lancaster B1, Waddington, England, May 1944. British bomber crew preparing to board their Lancaster for another mission. This aircraft was delivered in June 1942 and flew continuously on operations until the end of the war, completing 137 sorties.

USAAF Boeing B-17, Molesworth, England, April 1944.
Staff Sergeant Norman Sampson's cramped view as a B-17 ball turret gunner of the 303rd Bomb Group. Sampson and his crew joined the "Goldfish Club" (airmen who had survived a wartime aircraft ditching) on September 6, 1943, when their aircraft came down off the coast of England while returning from a raid on Stuttgart, Germany.

USAAF Boeing B-17F, Thurleigh, England, July 1943.
Lieutenant Stanley Stedt, bombardier in the 423rd Bomb Squadron, 306th Bomb Group, rides a 2,000lb bomb while gunners sit atop 0.50in caliber ammunition. Arriving in England in September 1942, the 306th was the longest continuously serving bomb group of the 8th Air Force during the war and led the first mission against Germany on January 27, 1943.

USAAF Consolidated B-24J, Attlebridge, England, date unknown. Groundcrew of the 466th Bomb Group prepare to install a new Pratt & Whitney R-1830 Twin Wasp engine on one of the group's Liberator bombers.

USAAF Consolidated B-24J, Attlebridge, England, date unknown. Armorers install tail fuzes on bombs next to a Liberator of the 784th Bomb Squadron, 466th Bomb Group.

USAAF Consolidated B-24J, Attlebridge, England, date unknown. A mechanic of the 466th Bomb Group services a Liberator's oxygen bottles.

 USAAF, Debden, England, 1944. Colonel Don Blakeslee began as a Spitfire pilot with the Royal Canadian Air Force, and later became a member of the RAF "Eagle" Squadron. When the US joined the war, the "Eagle" Squadrons were transferred to the USAAF as the 4th Fighter Group and there he flew P-47 Thunderbolts and P-51 Mustangs. A colonel at 26-years-old, Blakeslee flew more combat missions against the Luftwaffe than any other American fighter pilot (over 500 missions). He commanded the 4th Fighter Group from January 1, 1944 to September 1944, and was credited with 15.5 kills.

USAAF, Debden, England, 1944. Colonel Don Blakeslee, commander of the 4th Fighter Group, was extremely unhappy with the P-47, so he convinced the 8th Air Force command to give them Mustangs. They flew their first operational mission within 24 hours of receiving them, and Blakeslee told his pilots to "learn how to fly them on the way to the target." The 4th Fighter Group was the highest scoring Allied fighter group in the war, destroying 1,016 enemy aircraft.

 Luftwaffe Messerschmitt Bf 109G-6, Normandy, France, June 7, 1944. British troops inspect a Bf 109 that was shot down by USAAF P-47s the day after D-Day. Its pilot, Uffz Rudolf Strosetzki of 6./JG 11, crash landed near Tilly-sur-Seulles and became a POW for the rest of the war.

 RAF Hawker Typhoon Mk Ib, RAF Matlask, England, spring 1943. No 56 Squadron was the first to receive the Typhoon, known as the "Tiffy." This aircraft was assigned to Squadron Leader Thomas Henry Vicent "THV" Pheloung of New Zealand. While attacking a German convoy off the Dutch coast in June 1943, Pheloung's aircraft was hit by flak and plunged straight into the sea.

 USAAF, Boxted, England, July 1944. Lieutenant Colonel Francis S. "Gabby" Gabreski, commander of the 61st Fighter Squadron, 56th Fighter Group, poses with his groundcrew. Gabreski became the leading US ace in Europe with 28 kills.

 USAAF Boeing B-17G, Bassingbourn, England, April 1945. "Little Miss Mischief" of the 324th Bomb Squadron, 91st Bomb Group, comes to grief after returning early from a mission due to an engine failure (note the feathered propeller). Upon landing at Bassingbourn, its landing gear collapsed.

 USAAF Boeing B-17G, English Channel, 1945. The white cliffs of Dover were a welcome sight to returning aircrew after a long mission. "Anxious Angel," the closest aircraft, was assigned to the 401st Bomb Squadron, 91st Bomb Group, and flew over 70 missions. Below the tail is "Little Miss Mischief," which is also featured in the above photo. This B-17 carries unusual natural metal front fuselage joined with another aircraft's olive drab rear fuselage, after having been damaged by flak on an earlier mission.

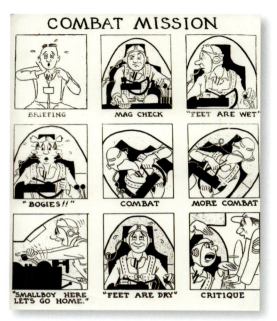

 USAAF Republic P-47D, Boxted, England, Fall 1944. Named "Silver Lady," this was the first unpainted Thunderbolt delivered to the 56th Fighter Group in May 1944. Assigned to seven-victory ace Major Leslie Smith of the 61st Fighter Squadron, who scored two or three kills in it. Lieutenant Colonel Francis "Gabby" Gabreski (28 kills) also flew "Silver Lady," scoring three kills on May 22, and two more on June 7, 1944.

 USAAF Lockheed F-5E, England, Fall 1944. Major Troy McGuire, commanding officer of the 22nd Photo Reconnaissance Squadron, 7th Photo Reconnaissance Group (PRG), in his F-5E nicknamed "Sis and Willie." The 7th PRG took more than three million intelligence photographs over Europe during the war.

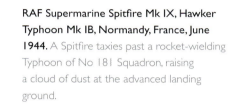

RAF Supermarine Spitfire Mk IX, Hawker Typhoon Mk IB, Normandy, France, June 1944. A Spitfire taxies past a rocket-wielding Typhoon of No 181 Squadron, raising a cloud of dust at the advanced landing ground.

USAAF, Halesworth, England, March 14, 1944. On "Brass Hats Day," top USAAF officers visited the 56th Fighter Group. Standing, left to right: Lieutenant Colonel David Schilling (56th Fighter Group Deputy Commander), Colonel Hub Zemke (56th Fighter Group Commander), Major General William Kepner (commander of the 8th Fighter Command), Brigadier General Jesse Auton (65th Fighter Wing commander). Sitting and admiring a Vargas pin-up: Major General Jimmy Doolittle (8th Air Force commander) and Lieutenant General Carl Spaatz (commander of US Strategic Air Forces in Europe).

USAAF Lockheed P-38, Normandy, France, June 1944. A P-38J Lightning of the 392nd Fighter Squadron, 367th Fighter Group, at the newly constructed airfield overlooking Omaha Beach, only eight days after the D-Day invasion.

 USAAF Boeing B-17G, Bassingbourn, England, January 30, 1944.
Lieutenant Howard Groombridge, navigator of "Old Faithful" of the
401st Bomb Squadron, 91st Bomb Group, poking his head through
the remains of the astrodome after the aircraft was damaged by
flak over Germany.

 USAAF Boeing B-17G, Schweinfurt, Germany, March 24, 1944.
B-17s of the 423rd Bomb Squadron, 306th Bomb Group, on their
way to bomb the ball-bearing plant at Schweinfurt, Germany.

 Luftwaffe Messerschmitt Me 109E-7, France, 1941. Oberstleutnant Adolf Galland,
commander of JG 26, climbs into his fighter. The Bf 109E-7, introduced in late
August 1940, solved the limited range of earlier versions with the ability to carry
an external fuel tank. After the invasion of the Soviet Union in 1941, JG 26 and
JG 2 were the only fighter groups in France to defend against RAF offensive fighter
sweeps and bomber attacks across northern Europe.

 RAF de Havilland Mosquito NF Mk II, Castle Camps, England, May 25, 1943. No 605 (County of Warwick) Squadron's commander, Wing Commander C. D. Tomalin, and his radar observer, Squadron Leader Bob Muir, about to start up their Mosquito NF Mk II for another night intruder mission. According to squadron records, they were "a deadly and efficient partnership" who attacked enemy airfields and transportation lines on the continent. Muir scored two air-to-air kills at night.

 USAAF Douglas C-47, Exeter, England, June 5, 1944. Colonel Robert Wolverton (Commanding Officer of the 3rd Battalion, 506th Parachute Infantry Regiment, 101st Airborne Division) and his Headquarters stick about to board their C-47 for their combat jump into Normandy on D-Day. This C-47 was named "Stoy Hora" and flown by Colonel Frank Krebs, commander of the 440th Troop Carrier Group, who led the 45-ship formation of C-47s. Four of these paratroopers, including Colonel Wolverton, would die the next day.

 USAAF Boeing B-17F, Framlingham, England, 1943. Ordnance men of the 390th Bomb Group load high explosive bombs in preparation for another mission. In the background, mechanics work on the engine of B-17F "Coy De Coy" of the 569th Bomb Squadron. This B-17 was lost on January 4, 1944 over the Netherlands, with all 10 crewmen becoming prisoners of war.

 USAAF, Ridgewell, England, December 1, 1944. Warmth for a cold English winter day, as a multitude of pin-up pictures adorns the wall of the 533rd Bomb Squadron's (381st Bomb Group) Quonset hut used as a barber shop.

 USAAF Boeing B-17F and Republic P-47D, Europe, Fall 1943. An iconic image of the scale of the bomber war over Europe, as contrails fill the clear, cold skies over Germany. P-47s weave in order to stay with the slower B-17s of the 390th Bomb Group. The closest B-17 is "Skippy," which would be lost over England on February 5, 1944 when the crew bailed out after an engine failure.

 USAAF Boeing B-17F, England, June 9, 1943. Captain Robert Morgan and crew of their B-17F "Memphis Belle" about to depart England to return to the USA for a war bond tour. The crew completed their 25th mission on May 17, 1943, and the "Memphis Belle" flew her 25th mission on May 19 (with a different crew). After the tour, Morgan completed 26 more missions in B-29s in the Pacific.

 Luftwaffe Focke-Wulf Fw 190A, France, 1944. The success of the Allied campaign for air superiority over the European continent was starkly seen on D-Day, with the Luftwaffe flying 172 sorties compared to the Allied 14,000 sorties.

 USAAF, Boxted, England, 1944. Captain Fred Christensen was a replacement pilot assigned to the 62nd Fighter Squadron, 56th Fighter Group, in the summer of 1943. On July 7, 1944, he became the first pilot in the 8th Air Force to shoot down six enemy aircraft on one mission. He went on to score a total of 21.5 kills.

 Luftwaffe Messerschmitt Bf 109G, Germany, date unknown. Luftwaffe ace Leutnant Gottfried Weiroster relaxes between sorties with his Bf109G-5/R6 "Red 3" of JG 50. Weiroster was credited with six victories in 19 missions, including three B-17s. He was shot down and killed over Jadebusen on November 26, 1943.

 RAF Bristol Beaufighter, location and date unknown. An RAF Beaufighter crew about to launch on another anti-shipping mission. The Beaufighter was well-suited for the task, being able to make precision attacks at wave-top heights with torpedoes, 60lb rockets and four 20mm cannons. Over 5,900 Beaufighters were built.

 RAF Bristol Beaufighter, North Sea, 1944. A swarm of Beaufighters of RAF Coastal Command strafe a minesweeper off the German island of Borkum.

 USAAF Consolidated B-24J, Attlebridge, England, date unknown. Local women watch mechanics of the 466th Bomb Group change the engine and propeller on a Liberator.

 USAAF North American P-51B, Debden, England, May 1944. Lieutenant Ralph "Kidd" Hofer of the 334th Fighter Squadron, 4th Fighter Group, with his Mustang and his dog Duke. Known for his lack of discipline, long hair, and wearing a football jersey over his uniform, Hofer was often at odds with Colonel Don Blakeslee, 4th Fighter Group commander. Credited with 15 kills, Hofer was killed during a shuttle mission near Mostar, Yugoslavia on July 2, 1944.

US Navy Grumman F6F-3N, USS *Solomons*, Atlantic Ocean, November 18, 1944. The USS *Solomons* was an escort carrier that conducted anti-submarine patrols in the Atlantic Ocean throughout 1944, its pilots sinking a German U-boat on June 15. Later that year, the *Solomons* began service qualifying Navy and Marine pilots in carrier landings. Here, one Navy pilot learns the difficulties of landing on a moving airfield!

US Navy Consolidated PB4Y-1, England, Fall 1943. The PB4Y-1 was a navalized version of the USAAF's B-24D that was used by VB-103 to hunt for German U-boats in the Bay of Biscay. Just after 0100hrs on November 12, 1943, this PB4Y-1, named "Calvert n' Coke," engaged submarine U-508. Neither were heard from again. A search the next day revealed two oil slicks about 5 miles apart. All 57 German sailors and 10 US Navy aircrew were killed.

USAAF Boeing B-17G, Bassingbourn, England, 1944. Assigned to the 91st Bomb Group on April 7, 1944, this Flying Fortress had three different names with three different squadrons. It flew as "Anne" with the 324th Bomb Squadron, "The Bloody Bucket" with the 401st Bomb Squadron, and finally as "Hikin' for Home" with the 322nd Bomb Squadron. Lieutenant David Hanst named it "Hikin' for Home" because "that was what we looked forward to after each target – hiking for home." The aircraft flew over 90 combat missions.

USAAF Douglas A-20, location and date unknown. A-20 Havocs of the 410th Bomb Group flying away from their smoking target somewhere in Europe. Almost 7,500 A-20s were built, and they saw use as both light bombers and night fighters.

USAAF Boeing B-17, Molesworth, England, September 28, 1944. An iconic scene of the air war in Europe as officers and men of the 303rd Bomb Group gather on the control tower to scan the sky for the first glimpses of their B-17s returning from a bombing mission. Unfortunately, on this day, the 303rd lost 11 of their 28 bombers (nine of them shot down in the first pass by German fighters), with an additional 13 aircraft damaged during the raid. That night, 91 beds at Molesworth were empty.

KNEEDING A LIFT

USAAF Consolidated B-24J, Attlebridge, England, date unknown. Groundcrew of the 466th Bomb Group repair a Liberator's vertical tail and rudder.

USAAF, Ridgewell, England, date unknown. Two aircrew relax with a cup of coffee by the fire in the 381st Bomb Group's Officer's Club. A B-17 group that flew combat missions from June 22, 1943 to April 25, 1945, the 381st suffered the highest losses of all bomber groups on the first mission to bomb the key industrial city of Schweinfurt on August 17, 1943, losing 11 out of 22 bombers

USAAF Republic P-47D, Boxted, England, 1944. Armorers reloading the eight .50in caliber machine guns of Lieutenant Colonel Francis "Gabby" Gabreski's 56th Fighter Group P-47D Thunderbolt.

Wehrmacht V-2, location and date unknown. The V-2 (German Vergeltungswaffe 2, or Retribution Weapon 2) was the world's first long-range guided ballistic missile. Beginning on September 8, 1944, over 3,100 V-2s were launched against Allied targets, causing the deaths of an estimated 9,000 civilians and military personnel.

USAAF North American P-51D, Kingscliffe, England, 1945. A local man paints Mustangs of the 79th Fighter Squadron, 20th Fighter Group, in their hardstands at Kingscliffe.

USAAF pilots, London, England, date unknown. Two pilots from the 56th Fighter Group survey the bomb damage around St Paul's Cathedral.

 USAAF Republic P-47D, Boxted, England, June 1944.
Lieutenant Colonel Francis S. "Gabby" Gabreski watches as a bomb is loaded on his Thunderbolt. "Gabby," only 25 years old, was scheduled to return to the USA in late July 1944. As he was about to get aboard the transport, he decided to fly one last mission. As he strafed a German airfield, he flew so low that his propeller hit the ground. He was forced to crash land and became a POW for the remainder of the war.

 USAAF Republic P-47D, Boxted, England, 1944.
"Shack Rat," a Thunderbolt of the 63rd Fighter Squadron, 56th Fighter Group, at its hardstand in England. Lieutenant Ramon Davis was flying a support mission over the Netherlands on September 26, 1944, when he ran out of gas and crash landed. The aircraft was a write-off.

 USAAF Republic P-47D, Chièvres, Belgium, late 1944. Captain George King of the 386th Fighter Squadron, 365th Fighter Group, taxies his P-47D Thunderbolt for another close air support mission. In the foreground is a quad .50in caliber machine gun emplacement. The aircraft was lost over Germany on May 17, 1945, killing its pilot Lieutenant Clarence E. Felker, Jr.

 USAAF North American P-51C, Fowlmere, England, January 16, 1945. Mustang of the 503rd Fighter Squadron, 339th Fighter Group, in its revetment. This Mustang has the modified Malcolm hood canopy and a field-installed fillet in front of the vertical stabilizer (to improve stability). Lieutenant Esteban Terrats was killed in action in this aircraft on March 2, 1945 while escorting bombers to Germany.

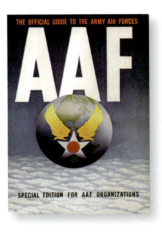

 USAAF, Molesworth, England, December 1942. Sergeant Henry Kwasneske of the 303rd Bomb Group checks an ammunition belt next to his B-17. The 303rd BG, known as the "Hell's Angels," flew more sorties than any other 8th Air Force B-17 group.

 USAAF Boeing B-17, Osnabruck, Germany, 1943. A 91st Bomb Group Flying Fortress over the target at 25,000ft. Bombing crews had to drop through the clouds owing to complete cloud cover. Note the lines on the bomber's wings and tail for the waist gunners to use as an aiming reference.

USAAF North American P-51D, Ober Olm, Germany, April 17, 1945. Lieutenant Colonel Glen Eagleston (18.5 aerial victories and commander of the 353rd Fighter Squadron) and Lieutenant Colonel Jack Bradley (15 kills and deputy commander of the 354th Fighter Group) brief pilots for another mission. Eagleston, 24-years-old at the time of this picture, was the leading ace of the 9th Air Force.

 USAAF Lockheed P-38, Belgium, December 19, 1944. Loaded with bombs, this P-38 Lightning of the 9th Air Force awaits its next close air support mission at a former Luftwaffe airbase in Belgium during the Battle of the Bulge.

Luftwaffe Dornier Do 335, Lechfield, Germany, July 1945. The fifth production model of the Do 335A-1 Pfeil (Arrow) was captured in April 1945. It had a unique push-pull engine configuration, which reduced drag and made it Germany's fastest piston-engine aircraft of the war. In the background is an Arado 234 Blitz, the world's first operational jet bomber.

Luftwaffe Messerschmitt Me 262A and Junkers Ju 87D, Innsbruck, Austria, 1945. The Me 262 Schwalbe (Swallow) was the world's first operational jet fighter, and had a 100mph advantage over rival fighters. The Allies found success in countering the jets by attacking them on the ground or in the traffic pattern preparing to land.

Luftwaffe Junkers Ju 88 and Focke-Wulf Fw 190, Germany, April/May 1945. US troops inspect a Mistel (German for mistletoe). A combination of two aircraft, the Mistel was the larger one filled with explosives (here, a Ju 88) that was flown by the pilot in the smaller aircraft (a Fw 190) before being released to hit its target. First flown in July 1943, about 250 were built using various aircraft combinations, but they had limited success.

 USAAF Douglas A-26B, Juvincourt, France, April 29, 1945. An Invader of the 647th Bomb Squadron, 410th Bomb Group, suffered a nose-gear collapse on landing. The 410th Bomb Group was assigned to the 9th Air Force and primarily flew Douglas A-20 Havocs before converting to the Invader late in the war.

 French AF Yakovlev Yak-3, Le Bourget, France, June 1945. Three American pilots and a Red Cross worker inspect a Yak-3 fighter that the Normandie-Niemen Escadrille brought back to France as a gift from the Soviet Union. The French pilot is ace Major Pierre Matras who joined the Normandie-Niemen regiment of French pilots fighting in Russia in May 1944.

 USAAF Boeing B-17G, Bassingbourn, England, April 1944. General Dwight D. Eisenhower, Supreme Commander of Allied Forces in Europe, meets the crew of a B-17G named in his honor from the 91st Bomb Group. "General Ike" received battle damage on several occasions, including on her 65th mission when flak severed the propeller from her number three engine (right inboard) and sliced through the fuselage. Miraculously no one was injured.

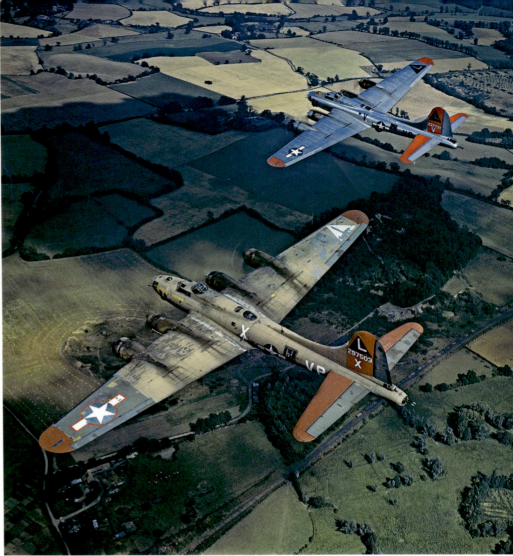

 USAAF Boeing B-17G, Bassingbourn, England, date unknown. The tail gunner at his station in "Ack Ack Annie" of the 322nd Bomb Squadron, 91st Bomb Group. The first natural metal aircraft assigned to the 91st Bomb Group, "Ack Ack Annie" flew a total of 143 combat missions, surviving the war.

 USAAF Boeing B-17G, England, 1944. A weathered camouflaged "Princess Pat" flies on the wing of a newer natural metal B-17G, both of the 533rd Bomb Squadron, 381st Bomb Group. The silver bomber was battle damaged on the December 18, 1944 mission to Cologne and force landed on the continent. "Princess Pat" crash landed at Ridgewell on March 26, 1945.

 USAAF Boeing B-17G, Rattlesden, England, date unknown. The bombardier's view of the 447th Bomb Group taxiing out for another bombing mission. Between December 24, 1943 and April 21, 1945 the 447th Bomb Group flew 258 combat missions over Europe.

 USAAF North American P-51D, Debden, England, March 24, 1945. Mustangs of the 336th Fighter Squadron, 4th Fighter Group, prepare to depart in support of the Allied crossing of the Rhine River. That day, a total of 1,158 P-47s and P-51s flew over the Rhine, claiming 53 German fighters for the loss of nine Mustangs.

 Luftwaffe Messerschmitt Bf 110G, Fritzlar, Germany, April 1945. Fellow 365th Fighter Group "Hell Hawks" pilots listen to 1st Lieutenant Robert Hagan talk about a dogfight while standing next to a captured Bf 110G-4 night fighter. Hagan flew 91 missions with the 386th Fighter Squadron.

CHAPTER EIGHT

WAR IN THE PACIFIC

The American planes looked like they had just rolled out of the factory; their blue polished wings flashed in the bright sunlight. It must have been great to fly those beautiful new machines with no worries about parts, supplies, or gasoline. I envied them. You see, we were running for our lives up there. The Hellcats were faster and outnumbered us ten to one. It doesn't matter how skilled a pilot is if he is outnumbered.

Toshimitsu Imaizumi, Imperial Japanese Navy, describing the air battles of October 15–16, 1944 over Saipan

We were in a right-hand turn — we had just shot down one plane — and as we turned I slid underneath and saw a Zero coming down directly at me. I pulled up and turned into him and squeezed the trigger and he just blew up. I normally flew with my canopy partially open and when I flew underneath the fireball I could feel the heat.

Ensign Rudolph Matz, US Navy, describing the first of two kills on June 19, 1944

When the Japanese attacked Pearl Harbor, they also launched simultaneous attacks on American bases in Wake Island, Guam, and the Philippines, invaded Thailand, and attacked the British possessions of Malaya, Singapore and Hong Kong. Despite the surprise attack on Pearl Harbor, the US fleet was not destroyed. The aircraft carriers were at sea during the attack, and vital infrastructure (such as the fuel and oil tanks) was relatively untouched.

Japan quickly seized natural resources in the Dutch East Indies and Malaya in order to escape the effects of the Allied embargo. The British warships HMS *Prince of Wales* and HMS *Repulse* were sunk by Japanese bombers and torpedo bombers on December 10, 1941, the first time battleships in the open sea were sunk solely by airpower. Hong Kong fell two weeks later, and Guam and Wake Island were also captured. In January 1942, the Japanese invaded Burma, the Dutch East Indies, New Guinea, and the Solomon Islands, and captured Manila, Kuala Lumpur and Rabaul. Singapore surrendered on February 15, 1942.

The first Japanese air attacks on Australia were on February 19, 1942 and later that month the Imperial Japanese Navy decisively defeated an Allied naval force at the Battle of the Java Sea. For a while, American and Filipino forces resisted the Japanese in the Philippines, until the final surrender at Corregidor on May 8, 1942.

On April 18, 1942, 16 USAAF B-25s led by Lieutenant Colonel Jimmy Doolittle took off from the USS *Hornet* in a mostly symbolic attack on Japan that greatly boosted American morale.

Allied codebreakers discovered the Japanese were planning to attack Port Moresby, New Guinea, and the resulting Battle of the Coral Sea in May 1942 was the first naval battle in history where the ships involved never saw each other. Although considered a tactical victory for the Japanese, the Allies prevented a Japanese invasion of Port Moresby and won a strategic victory. Japanese losses in ships, aircraft and pilots diminished their strength in the upcoming Battle of Midway.

Erroneously believing the US Navy was down to its last two aircraft carriers, the Japanese planned to lure the fleet into a trap. A diversionary force sailed north and captured the Aleutian Islands of Kiska and Attu, while the main Japanese fleet arrived off Midway on June 4, 1942, surprised that three US aircraft carriers were waiting for them. The Japanese lost four aircraft carriers and many highly-trained pilots in the battle, which proved to be a turning point in the Pacific War.

Japanese forces continued their advance in the Solomon Islands and New Guinea in the summer of 1942, but on August 7, Allied forces led by US Marines landed on Guadalcanal, which was eventually recaptured following months of hard-fought battles.

In order to neutralize the major Japanese base at Rabaul, the Allies devised a military strategy known as island-hopping, using submarine and air attacks to isolate Japanese bases that the Allies decided to bypass. US Navy Admiral Chester Nimitz would lead the northern thrust through the Gilbert and Marshall Islands, the Marianas and Okinawa, while US Army General Douglas MacArthur would attack through the southwest Pacific islands of the Solomons, New Guinea, and the Philippines.

On June 15, 1944, the Allies invaded Saipan in order to capture airfields from which B-29s could attack Japan. The ensuing naval battle on June 19–20, was the largest carrier-to-carrier battle in history. Known as the Battle of the Philippine Sea, or the "Great Marianas Turkey Shoot," the Japanese lost three carriers and over 400 aircraft. An even larger naval battle took place on October 23–26, 1944 in the Battle of Leyte Gulf. Notable as the largest naval battle in World War II, the last time in history that battleships engaged each other, and the first Japanese use of kamikazes, the Allied victory established air and sea superiority in the western Pacific.

Following the recapture of the Philippines, the largest and bloodiest American battle began with the invasion of Okinawa on April 1, 1945. Increasing Japanese use of kamikaze attacks resulted in 38 ships sunk and 368 more damaged.

The world changed forever on August 6, 1945 when a B-29 named "Enola Gay" dropped an atomic bomb on Hiroshima. Three days later, another B-29 dropped an atomic bomb on Nagasaki.

On August 15, 1945, the Japanese emperor broadcast to his people and the world the Japanese surrender, known as V-J Day (Victory in Japan). The formal surrender was signed on September 2, 1945, ending World War II six years and one day after it began.

 USN Grumman F6F-3, USS *Lexington*, November 23, 1943. A Hellcat of Fighting Squadron Sixteen (VF-16) gets the take-off flag from Lieutenant John M. Clark during operations in the Gilberts and Marshalls. VF-16 pilots shot down 17 Japanese aircraft during the missions.

 USN Grumman F4F-3, USS *Enterprise*, October 28, 1941. Mechanics assemble a Fighting Squadron Three (VF-3, "Felix the Cat") Wildcat on the hangar deck with Douglas TBD-1 Devastator torpedo planes of Torpedo Squadron Three (VT-3) and Douglas SBD Dauntless dive bombers of Scouting Squadron Two (VS-2) hanging overhead.

 USN Douglas SBD, USS _Enterprise_, August 7, 1942. Ordnancemen of Scouting Squadron Six (VS-6) load a 500lb bomb on an SBD Dauntless dive bomber on the deck of the USS _Enterprise_ on the first day of air strikes against Guadalcanal and Tulagi.

 USMC Grumman F4F-3, Midway, June 1942. A damaged and partially disassembled Wildcat of Marine Fighting Squadron 221 (VMF-221) on Sand Island, Midway Atoll. On the early morning of June 4, 27 fighter pilots of VMF-221, flying a mix of Brewster F2A-3 Buffalos and Wildcats, attacked the 108 incoming Japanese aircraft, losing 13 Buffalos and three Wildcats in the process. This Wildcat was flown by Captain John Carey, who shot down a Japanese bomber but was wounded in the fight.

USAAF Consolidated B-24, Marshall Islands, 1944. Hollywood actress Betty Hutton making a morale-boosting USO tour visit to B-24 mechanics on an airfield in the Marshall Islands.

USMC Vought F4U-1, location unknown, September 1943. The Corsair, famous for its inverted gull wings and high speed, was used by the US Marines and Navy to great success.

 USN Grumman F6F, location and date unknown. Mechanics salvage what they can from a wrecked Hellcat aboard a carrier in the Pacific. They have lashed down the aircraft to the deck to help secure it, and will soon move on to another wrecked aircraft.

 USN Grumman F6F-3, USS *Yorktown,* **August 31, 1943.** The Commander Air Group Five, Lieutenant Commander James Flatley, in his Hellcat preparing to lead the attack on Marcus Island. Awarded the Navy Cross for his actions during the May 1942 Battle of the Coral Sea, Flatley was an ace with six kills.

 USN Vought OS2U-3, USS *Baltimore*, February 18, 1944. A Kingfisher is recovered by the heavy cruiser USS *Baltimore* after Lieutenant (junior grade) Denver Baxter and his radioman Reuben Hickman rescued Fighting Squadron Nine (VF-9) Hellcat pilot Lieutenant (junior grade) George Blair. Blair was shot down by flak during the dawn fighter sweep over Truk Lagoon.

 USN Grumman F6F-5, USS *Essex*, December 1, 1944. Pilots of Fighting Squadron Fifteen (VF-15) at the end of their six-month tour of duty in the Pacific, during which they shot down 310 Japanese aircraft. Lieutenant Commander James Rigg, VF-15 Commanding Officer and ace with 11 kills, is to the left of the score card. Commander David McCampbell, Commander Air Group 15, is standing to the right of the score card, and his Hellcat "Minsi III" is in the background. McCampbell was the Navy's leading ace with 34 kills, nine of them on a single sortie on October 24, 1944, and was awarded the Medal of Honor.

 USAAF Northrop P-61A, Saipan, 1944. Pilot 1st Lieutenant Francis "Lil Ab" Eaton, radar operator 2nd Lieutenant James Ketchum, and gunner Staff Sergeant William Anderson III, shot down a Japanese "Betty" bomber in "Nightie Mission" on July 7, 1944. This P-61A of the 6th Night Fighter Squadron was lost on August 5, 1945, owing to damage from a typhoon.

 USAAF Northrop P-61A, Saipan, September 1944. A Black Widow of the 6th Night Fighter Squadron being readied for a mission from Saipan, Mariana Islands. The P-61 was the first American aircraft designed with airborne radar, and the antenna can be seen through the partially transparent radome. The crew of "Midnight Mickey," pilot Lieutenant Myrle McCumber, radar operator Flight Officer Daniel Hinz, and gunner/mechanic Private Peter Dutkanicz, scored two of the squadron's 16 air-to-air kills.

 USN General Motors FM-2, USS *Petrof Bay*, March 25, 1945.
FM-2 Wildcats of composite squadron VC-93 prepare for a
mission supporting the invasion of Okinawa.

 At sea, location and date unknown. In time-honored
tradition, shipmates bury a fallen comrade at sea.

 USMC Vought F4U-1A, Bougainville, December 1943. VMF-214, commanded by Major Greg "Pappy" Boyington, started operating from Torokina Field, Bougainville, as a forward staging base on December 11, 1943. In that month, the "Black Sheep" flew 900 combat sorties, shooting down 32 Japanese aircraft.

 USAAF Republic P-47D, Saipan, 1944. Pilots of the 73rd Fighter Squadron, 318th Fighter Group, brief for another dive bombing mission against Japanese-held Pagan in the Marianas. 1st Lieutenant Julius Smith and Major John Hussey, Jr (three victories) are pointing at the map.

 USAAF Republic P-47D, Saipan, July 1944. Loaded with two 1,000lb bombs, Major Henry McAfee's Thunderbolt of the 19th Fighter Squadron, 318th Fighter Group, was one of the last "razorbacks" built. On June 22, 1944, 24 Thunderbolts of the 19th Fighter Squadron launched from the carrier USS *Natoma Bay* to land on Saipan, where the squadron immediately began supporting the Marines.

 USAAF Lockheed P-38J, Guadalcanal, early 1944. A P-38J Lightning of the 44th Fighter Squadron put to practical use as a laundry dryer in the sunny heat on Guadalcanal. The aircraft would be written off in a crash in New Guinea in February 1945.

 USAAF Lockheed P-38E, Aleutians, 1942. Captains Howard Millard and Arthur Hustead of the 54th Fighter Squadron discuss their mission in the Aleutian Islands. Owing to the inhospitable nature of the region, more pilots were lost due to weather rather than combat.

 USAAF Curtiss P-40K, Amchitka, October 12, 1943.
On Amchitka, Aleutian Islands, a groundcrew repairs P-40K Warhawk "Dell" of the 18th Fighter Squadron, while "Flaming Mame" awaits its turn.

 USAAF, Aleutians, Fall 1942. Captain Morgan Giffin, commander of the 54th Fighter Squadron, shows the combined wear and tear of combat and the harsh climate of the Aleutians. Twelve of the squadron's original 25 pilots were dead within a year of deploying to Alaska. Giffin shot down a "Jake" seaplane in early 1943 and survived the war, but died in 1945 in the crash of a C-45 in Nebraska.

USN General Motors FM-2, USS *Gambier Bay*, August 1, 1944. Ensign Darrell "Smokey" Bennet by his well-worn Wildcat of Composite Squadron Ten (VC-10). Two months after this picture, he survived the sinking of the *Gambier Bay*, the only US Navy carrier sunk by naval gunfire during the war.

USN Grumman F4F-4, USS *Ranger*, Fall 1942. Wildcats of Fighting Squadron Nine (VF-9) on the deck of the USS *Ranger* during a work-up cruise.

 USN General Motors TBM, location and date unknown. Flames from the burning fuel of a sinking Avenger rise to the surface. Grumman began to phase out production of the TBF Avenger in 1943, and General Motors began producing it as the TBM.

 USAAF Boeing B-29s, Marianas, 1944. B-29 Superfortress bombers of the 869th Bomb Squadron, 497th Bomb Group, flying a practice formation flight. The lead bomber is "Dauntless Dotty," flown by Major Robert Morgan, who completed 25 missions over Europe in the B-17 "Memphis Belle." In "Dauntless Dotty," Morgan led the first B-29 bombing mission against Tokyo on November 24, 1944, the first since the Doolittle raid of April 1942.

 Imperial Japanese Navy Mitsubishi A6M3 Type 32, Papua New Guinea, December 27, 1942. This A6M3 Type 32 "Hamp" was captured at Buna Airfield. The Type 32's square wing-tips made US intelligence think it was a totally new aircraft, so they designated it the "Hap" after USAAF Chief of Staff General Hap Arnold. He was not impressed, so it was quickly renamed "Hamp," but eventually it was realized it was a modified "Zeke," so it became the "Zeke 32." However, pilots generally referred to all versions of the A6M as the "Zero."

Imperial Japanese Navy Mitsubishi A6M5, location unknown, 1944. Although the A6M5 Type 52 Zero was not very fast, it had incredible range and maneuverability. "Never turn with a Zero" was the motto of Allied fighter pilots.

USAAF Consolidated B-24J, Angaur Island, November 24, 1944. "Kuuipo" (sweetheart in Hawaiian) of the 864th Bomb Squadron, 494th Bomb Group was a veteran of 45 combat missions when it was attacked by Japanese fighters on July 25, 1945 during a raid over Ryukyu Island. Although badly damaged, it flew on for another two hours before exploding inflight. Only two of the 11 crew members survived.

IJAAF Mitsubishi Ki-46 II, China, date unknown. Nicknamed "Dinah" by the Allies, the Ki-46 was a fast, high-altitude reconnaissance aircraft that proved difficult for fighters to intercept. Mitsubishi built 1,742 "Dinahs."

 USN Douglas SBD, Wake Island, October 1943. A flight of SBD Dauntless dive bombers from Bombing Squadron Five (VB-5) from the USS *Yorktown*. SBDs sank more enemy shipping in the war in the Pacific than any other Allied bomber.

 Imperial Japanese Navy, 1944. Survivors of a Japanese destroyer cling to their ship as it starts to sink.

 USAAF North American B-25J, North Borneo, April 1945. Japanese machine gun bullets splash in the water as the Mitchell bomber of the 42nd Bomb Group speeds away from a tree-top bombing and strafing attack on the seaplane base at Victoria Harbor. 2nd Lieutenant Russell Brown successfully evaded the anti-aircraft fire to bring his aircraft and crew safely back to base.

 USAAF Sikorsky YR-4B and North American B-25J, Burma, February 5, 1945. A Whirlaway helicopter hovers over a wrecked Mitchell bomber, which has been painted with a large X on its wing to prevent other pilots reporting the crash as a new one. The R-4 was the only helicopter to see active service in World War II, and was the first US rotary-wing aircraft to be mass produced.

 USMC Vought F4U-1A, Vella Lavella, December 1943. A Corsair of VMF-214, commanded by Major Gregory "Pappy" Boyington, in the south Pacific. Boyington often flew this aircraft, but it was lost when it ran out of fuel and ditched off-shore from Malekula Island.

USN Curtiss SB2C-4, location and date unknown. Developed to replace the Douglas SBD Dauntless, the Helldiver was a much larger aircraft. It carried bombs internally and had under-wing stations for rockets, but suffered from poor handling qualities. Pilots called it the "Beast."

USN Grumman F6F-3, USS *Yorktown*, circa November 1943. Sailors watch a movie while ordnancemen work on loading bombs onto Hellcats of Fighting Squadron Five (VF-5). This was likely taken during *Yorktown's* participation in Task Force 50's assault on the Gilbert Islands.

USN Grumman F6F, USS *Essex*, 1944. Lieutenant (junior grade) James Duffy (an ace with five kills) takes off in his Fighter Squadron Fifteen (VF-15) Hellcat. On June 19, 1944, in what became known as "The Marianas Turkey Shoot," VF-15 shot down 69 enemy aircraft, a one-day record that has never been equaled by any other American fighter squadron.

 USN, USS _Enterprise_, February 17, 1944.
Fighting Squadron Ten (VF-10) Hellcat
pilots share a laugh with their Air Group
Commander, Commander William "Killer"
Kane (seated far right, credited with six
kills) after attacking Truk Lagoon. Lieutenant
(junior grade) Joseph "Frenchy" Reulet
(seated second from left) had just become
an ace when he shot down three Zeros
over Truk. Lieutenant (junior grade) Philip
Kirkwood (seated third from left) was
credited with four kills in Hellcats, and
shot down another eight aircraft after the
squadron converted to the F4U Corsair.

 USN Douglas SBD-5, USS _Yorktown_, 1943.
A Dauntless dive bomber moving into
position for take-off. At the Battle of Midway
in June 1942, four squadrons of SBDs sank
or fatally damaged all four Japanese carriers,
changing the course of the War in the Pacific.

 **Imperial Japanese Navy Yokosuka MXY-7,
Okinawa, 1945.** Attached underneath a
modified Mitsubishi G4M2 "Betty" bomber,
then released and flown into the target
by a kamikaze pilot, the Ohka (Cherry
Blossom) could reach a speed of 600mph
after igniting its rocket boosters. On March
21, 1945, during the invasion of Okinawa,
the Japanese launched 16 "Bettys" carrying
Ohkas. US Navy Hellcats shot down the
entire bomber force before any Ohkas
were released.

 USN and USMC Vought F4U-1D, USS *Bunker Hill*, April 1945.
Three squadrons of Corsairs aboard *Bunker Hill* – Navy
Fighting Squadron Eighty-Four (VF-84) and the two Marine
Corps squadrons (VMF-221 and VMF-451) used these
aircraft interchangeably. On May 11, 1945, while off Okinawa,
two Japanese kamikazes struck the *Bunker Hill*, with a bomb
penetrating VF-84's ready room, killing 22 members of the unit.

 USN Grumman F6F-3, USS *Enterprise*, November 10, 1943.
When the right gear of Ensign Byron Johnson's Hellcat collapsed
on landing, the external fuel tank started leaking fuel and sparks
from the still-turning propeller hitting the flight deck set the
aircraft aflame. The catapult officer, Lieutenant Walter Chewning,
ran to assist Johnson out of the aircraft. Both men survived the
flames, and Johnson went on to score eight kills with VF-2 during
the invasion of Iwo Jima in 1944.

USN Douglas SBD, location and date unknown. Affectionately nicknamed "Slow But Deadly" by its crews, the SBD did not have folding wings in order to incorporate a stronger wing spar to endure the stress of high-g pull-outs from dive bombing runs.

USN, USS *Bunker Hill*, May 11, 1945. Off the coast of Okinawa, two Japanese kamikazes hit within 30 seconds, destroying many parked aircraft full of fuel and ammunition, and killing 389 sailors and wounding 264. The sailor in the left foreground holding his helmet down over his ears had served most of the war on the ship's island. The day before the attack, he had been transferred to the ship's bow – every man at his old position was killed.

IJAAF Kawasaki Ki-61, Chofu Air Base Japan, Spring 1945. A Ki-61 Hien (Flying Swallow) of the 244th Sentai, which was primarily responsible for defending Tokyo. The Ki-61, known as "Tony" by the Allies because it resembled an Italian aircraft, was powered by a Kawasaki license-built Daimler Benz DB 601 engine (as used on the German Messerschmitt Bf 109).

 USAAF North American P-51D, Iwo Jima, July 1945. This photo was taken through the side window of a B-29 bomber that was leading these P-51s of the 458th Fighter Squadron, 506th Fighter Group on a long-range mission to Japan. On one such raid the 506th shot down 10 Japanese fighters. Captain Peter Norwick (in the closest aircraft) was credited with two victories.

 USAAF North American P-51D, Iwo Jima, March 1945. VLR (Very Long Range) Mustangs of the 531st Fighter Squadron, 21st Fighter Group, await their next mission over the Japanese homeland. Flying 675 miles from Iwo Jima to Japan and back again, VLR Mustang pilots were in their single-engine, single-seat airplane for over eight hours, most of it over the vast expanse of the Pacific Ocean.

 USAAF North American P-51D, Iwo Jima, July 1945. Lieutenant Ceil Dennis of the 45th Fighter Squadron, 15th Fighter Group, carrying the equipment a VLR Mustang pilot needed: parachute, lifebelt, life raft, seat, survival vest, helmet and goggles. Lieutenant Dennis was only 21 years old when the war ended.

 USN Grumman F6F-5, USS *Randolph*, 1945. Wearing distinctive tail stripes and all-white ailerons, the Hellcats of VF-/VBF-12 are about to be catapulted into the air. The combined squadron consisted of nearly 60 aircraft, which shot down 125 aircraft in five months in Japanese home waters.

 USAAF Boeing B-29, Tinian, July 1945. "Enola Gay" of the 393rd Bomb Squadron, 509th Composite Group, was flown by Colonel Paul Tibbets, Jr on the August 6, 1945 mission to Hiroshima. At 08.15:17 (Japan local time), the "Enola Gay" dropped the "Little Man" atomic bomb from 31,000ft and 44.4 seconds later, the world changed forever.

 Imperial Japanese Navy Mitsubishi G4M, Ie Shima, August 19, 1945. A delegation of 16 military and civilian representatives, led by the Vice Chief of the Japanese Army General Staff Lieutenant General Torashirou Kawabe, flew to Ie Shima in two specially painted "Betty" bombers (white with green crosses to clearly identify them). They then flew to the Philippines in a Douglas C-54 to meet with General Douglas MacArthur to sign Japan's formal surrender. The world war that had started six years earlier on the Polish border was finally over.

 Nagasaki, 1945. The devastation caused by the atomic bomb brought an end to the war in the Pacific.

COUNTLESS SOULS FLEW EXTRAORDINARY MACHINES

HIGH INTO AN ENDLESS BLUE – BORN OF WAR

THEY DID BATTLE FOR FREEDOM AND JUST CAUSE.

ONLY SOME WERE TO RETURN.

TIME DOES NOT DIM THE LIGHT OF HEROES,

THEIR STORY AND SACRIFICE LIVE ON. WE HONOR THEM.

INDEX